NUMBER TWENTY-FIVE:
The Walter Prescott Webb Memorial Lectures

Essays on
The French Revolution:
Paris and the Provinces

[THE WALTER PRESCOTT WEBB MEMORIAL LECTURES]

Essays on
The French Revolution:
Paris and the Provinces

BY STEVEN G. REINHARDT,
CLARKE GARRETT, RODERICK PHILLIPS,
NANCY FITCH, AND DONALD SUTHERLAND

Introduction by Robert Forster
Edited by Steven G. Reinhardt
and Elisabeth A. Cawthon

Published for the University of Texas at Arlington by
Texas A&M University Press: College Station

Library of Congress Cataloging-in-Publication Data

Essays on the French Revolution : Paris and the provinces / by Steven G.
   Reinhardt . . . [et al.] ; introduction by Robert Forster ; edited by
   Steven G. Reinhardt and Elisabeth A. Cawthon. — 1st ed.
      p.   cm. — (The Walter Prescott Webb memorial lectures ; 25)
   ISBN 0-89096-498-X (alk. paper)
     1. France — History — Revolution, 1789–1799.   I. Reinhardt,
Steven G., 1949– .   II. Cawthon, Elisabeth A., 1957– .   III. Series.
DC142.E85   1992
944.04 — dc20   91-22146
                                                  CIP

To Homer L. Kerr,
friend and colleague

Contents

Preface

ON THE OCCASION of the twenty-fifth annual Walter Prescott Webb Memorial Lectures, scholars of French history gathered at the University of Texas at Arlington to consider how and why people in the French provinces reacted to the decade of revolution initiated by Parisians in 1789. Participants in the lecture series of March 15, 1990, described how men and women across France sometimes welcomed, frequently modified, but most often rejected the policies emanating from Paris, thereby propelling the revolution along its fateful course. The present volume contains the results of their research. While the authors may differ in their approach and, in some respects, their conclusions, they essentially agree on the importance of understanding the French Revolution as a complex, continuing process of interaction between Paris and the provinces. They thereby offer a fresh appraisal of this revolutionary decade, one that emphasizes the extent to which provincial history supplies the key to understanding the dynamic of the French Revolution.

The contributors to the volume are drawn from across the continent, from the eastern seaboard and Canada to Texas and California. Each is a recognized scholar in French history. Robert Forster, author of the introduction, is professor of history at Johns Hopkins University and an acknowledged dean of eighteenth-century French historical studies. He has authored three major monographs: *The Nobility of Toulouse in the Eighteenth Century*, *The House of Saulx-Tavanes*, and *Merchants, Landlords, Magistrates: The Depont Family in Eighteenth-Century France*. With Orest Ranum, he coedited seven volumes containing selections from the noted French journal *Annales: Economies, Sociétés, Civilisations*. Currently he is investigating French colonial sugar planters and plantations in the Antilles.

Steven G. Reinhardt, assistant professor of history at the University of Texas at Arlington, is the author of *Justice in the Sarladais*,

1770–1790 and has published articles and reviews on crime and the criminal justice system in early modern France in *The Journal of Interdisciplinary History* and *European History Quarterly*.

Roderick Phillips is a recognized authority on the history of marriage and divorce. He has taught at universities in New Zealand, England, and Sweden and is currently associate professor of history at Carleton University in Canada. A prolific author who has contributed at least nine articles to American, British, Canadian, and French journals, Professor Phillips has written three books: *Family Breakdown in Late Eighteenth-Century France, Divorce in New Zealand: A Social History*, and the highly acclaimed recent work, *Putting Asunder: A History of Divorce in Western Society*.

Clarke Garrett, Charles A. Dana Professor at Dickinson College in Pennsylvania, is the author of numerous scholarly articles on the subject of popular religion and religious movements in the era of the French Revolution. Most recently, he has written *Spirit Possession and Popular Religion from the Camisards to the Shakers*. He earlier authored *Respectable Folly: Millenarians and the French Revolution in France and England*.

Nancy Fitch, winner of the Webb lectures essay competition, is assistant professor of history at California State University in Fullerton. A noted expert on the use of quantitative methods in history, she has served for several years as organizer and instructor at the Newberry Library's Summer Institute on Family and Community History. She has published "Statistical Fantasies and Historical Facts: History in Crisis and Its Methodological Implications" in *Historical Methods* and is soon to publish the results of her research on the reception of the revolution in central France.

Donald Sutherland, professor of history at the University of Maryland, is a noted authority on the French Revolution. He has traveled around the world to present his work at scholarly conferences, and, during the bicentennial celebration of the French Revolution, acted as consultant to the Smithsonian Institution and as advisor to *National Geographic*. In addition to his numerous journal articles, he is the author of *The Chouans: The Social Origins of Counter-Revolution in Upper Brittany, 1770–1796* and the widely acclaimed *France, 1789–1815: Revolution and Counterrevolution*.

Elisabeth A. Cawthon, coeditor of this volume with Steven G.

Reinhardt, is assistant professor of history at the University of Texas at Arlington. A specialist in British and American legal history, she published an article entitled "New Life for the Deodand" in the *American Journal of Legal History* and has written an essay on "The Guiteau Case and Anglo-American Insanity Law" for the *Encyclopedia of American Court Cases.*

On behalf of the UTA history department, the editors would like to acknowledge several benefactors of the Webb lectures. C. B. Smith, Sr., an Austin businessman and former student of Walter Prescott Webb, generously established the Webb Endowment Fund and made possible the publication of the lectures. Jenkins and Virginia Garrett of Fort Worth have long shown both loyalty and generosity to UTA. Recently the Webb lecture series has received major support from the Rudolf Hermanns' Endowment for the Liberal Arts. Dr. Wendell Nedderman, president of UTA, was instrumental in obtaining such funding and has always been a steadfast supporter of the lecture series. We would also like to acknowledge the assistance of Kenneth Philp, chairman of the history department, and the dedication of Stephen Maizlish, chairman of the Webb lectures committee. Finally, the editors wish to thank the individual authors for the warmth of their companionship during the lecture series and for the excellence of their contributions to this volume.

Steven G. Reinhardt
Elisabeth A. Cawthon

Essays on
The French Revolution

ROBERT FORSTER

Introduction: The French Revolution in the Provinces

NO FEWER THAN TEN major works of synthesis have appeared in commemoration of the bicentennial of the French Revolution. Of these ten, only those by Bergeron and Mayaud, Lucas and Lewis, Sutherland, and Vovelle have given extensive treatment to the Revolution in the provinces.[1] The overwhelming attention to Paris is not new of course. Most of the revolutionary historiography of the past two centuries from Alexis de Tocqueville and Jules Michelet to Alphonse Aulard and Albert Mathiez, has made the capital the center of interpretation. There were exceptions. Georges Lefebvre devoted much of his scholarly work to the peasants and the Revolution. Even more important was the fact that Lefebvre urged all historians of France under the Old Regime to begin their research with a local study. Furthermore, after World War II, researchers following the lead of Marxist historians Albert Soboul and Michel Vovelle and *Annaliste* historians Pierre Goubert and Emmanuel Le Roy Ladurie began to analyse social structure in the provinces (usually with quantitative tools), with differing views of the significance of the French Revolution.

In the last decade there has been another shift in the interpretation of the French Revolution. It has brought with it a new bundle of research techniques, relying much less on sociology, economics, and demography and much more on intellectual history, literary criticism, and discourse analysis.[2] Both the new interpretive model and the new techniques have once again made Paris the center of attention. The new interpretation focuses on an intellectual dynamic that makes the Reign of Terror the centerpiece of the revolutionary process. This "process" is best extrapolated or decoded for Paris, where there is a well-known chronology of political events and a gallery of personalities already in hand on which to build the new interpretive edifice. Moreover, the sources for a textual and symbolic analysis—for example, speeches, laws, remonstrances, legal briefs, newspapers, pamphlets, processions, and artistic expression (from painting to sculpture) — are available in much greater density in Paris, not to mention the greater facility of conducting research in the Mecca-on-the-Seine.

Of course the new techniques, to which one should add symbolic and cultural anthropology, are a net gain to Clio's arsenal, notwithstanding a certain discomfort among historians of a more positivist persuasion. Indeed since World War II "political culture" had been submerged, in France at least, by social analysis, even at times by a naive belief that quantitative precision was closer to historical objectivity. However, there is no reason why the old and new techniques cannot be mutually supportive. As Donald Sutherland's article in this collection makes clear, the historian must identify and chart an interplay between the social and geographic environment and the political culture. Moreover, the historian must demonstrate a matrix of linkages between the more stable social, economic, and cultural system or structure on one side *and* the more dynamic (in the case of the French Revolution) political culture on the other. In addition, one should always be aware of contingency, the unexpected consequences of an action, and cultural continuities often hidden behind the noise and glitter of revolutionary rhetoric and movement.

This collection of articles on the Revolution in the provinces is therefore welcome and salutary. The authors apply both new and old techniques to the process of revolution. The historian at the provincial level is keenly aware of structures for a number of reasons. Peasant France does not lend itself to the same level of rhetorical or ideological analysis that one can apply to the speeches of the National Convention in Paris, for example. The thought processes of a sharecropper from Nièvres or Vitré are much different from those of a *sans-culotte* from the Saint-Antoine quarter of Paris, not to speak of a Robespierre. The historian of a rural culture is more likely to be aware of those social, economic, and cultural (especially religious) structures that condition and distort any linear ideological dynamic. The more literate provincial town, though lending itself more readily to an analysis of ideologies of a Parisian stamp, has its own cultural traditions, as Clarke Garrett's article makes very clear. Perhaps because most of us are less familiar with a given provincial environment compared to Paris, it must be laid out for us, so that we are less likely to forget such mundane matters as rural geography, land tenure and seigneurial rights, the relation of town and country, religiosity, and marriage.

This is not to say that rhetoric and symbol are inessential parts of the puzzle, or that properly interpreted, they cannot enlighten us about the nature of the revolutionary process. All five authors are well aware of the importance of cultural and symbolic anthropology as one way to elucidate their story. They are also very insistent on the complexity of their case studies, on how the "sound and fury" of revolutionary agents or Jacobin converts, or even the slow implementation of a new legal system, can encounter that hard rock of customary behavior contemporaries might have called "fanaticism" or "God's will." The historian will use more refined labels — sense of community, suspicion of the outsider, unfulfilled promises, latent anti-Protestantism, male dominance in the household — as building blocks toward an overall explanation of the reaction of provincials to a national revolution that somehow was not entirely their own.

Each of the five articles presented here is distinct in focus and approach. Nevertheless, a number of themes or general concerns pervade some, if not all of them. First is the continuity of local values and traditions, and the surfacing or reassertion of such values when outsiders challenged them abruptly or insensitively. Second are the practical obstacles to application of new laws due partly to the lack of informed or convinced administrative personnel and partly to the very complexity of the local society. A single law, the Maximum, for example, would placate some citizens, anger others, and create ambivalence for still others. Third, as all historians know, the Revolution raised expectations. How these expectations were satisfied, unfulfilled, or distorted is traced and made understandable in the provincial context. What did "counterrevolution" mean to contemporaries and how useful is it as an explanatory device for historians? How can we relate the interests and values of various social groups to the revolutionary rhetoric and policies filtered through local Jacobin leaders and clubs? Both of these guiding questions are implicit in most of these studies.

Steven Reinhardt's article takes us to the villages of the Dordogne Valley through the eyes of thirty-five parish priests in the first winter of the Revolution. By March, 1790, the peasants of the Périgord began to take the legislation of August 4, 1789, seriously. District elections raised expectations more than the Great Fear had done the summer before. Reinhardt's main concern is to examine how traditional rites of violence in this region — going back to the seventeenth century — were related to outbreaks of peasant violence in early 1790. In brief, Reinhardt argues for a continuity in the use of symbols, although not necessarily the same symbols. He also finds discontinuity, however, reflected in less actual violence against persons, as well as a legalistic awareness of property claims and a demand for recognition of peasant dignity, especially from the "former seigneur."

Reinhardt's article is especially effective in conveying the immediacy of the peasant actions against local châteaux. We learn not only of the numbers of peasants assembled by church bells (up to a maximum of five thousand from eleven parishes) and the occupations of their leaders, but also of their behavior, goals, and even their words as they pulled down seigneurial weathervanes and replaced them with maypoles. Peasants demanded the removal of all signs of seigneurialism, from gallows and grain measures to church pews, as well as the restitution of dues collected since August 4 and their titles to such seigneurial dues. Perhaps most important, they demanded that the seigneur or his agent legitimize these actions by providing a village banquet and performing the "fraternal embrace." The author suggests that the timing of these revolts was not unrelated to the carnival season and Mikhail Bakhtin's principle of inversion, yet he also acknowledges the differences between these revolts and their seventeenth-century predecessors. Reinhardt demonstrates on the village level the adaptation of traditional gestures and symbols to a new situation. Although his story does not take us beyond 1790, it is clear that the peasantry of the Périgord had replaced the traditional *jacquerie* with a rural revolution that bypassed the legislation from Paris. Georges Lefebvre would applaud this kind of local history; it is in the tradition of his classic work, *The Great Fear.*

Clarke Garrett's study also evokes the continuity of earlier conflict, this time going back to the Reformation. Despite the apparent decline of religious strife between Protestant and Catholic in the eighteenth century, Garrett demonstrates how fragile religious tolerance was in the towns of the Garonne Valley, Toulouse and Montauban in particular. After a summary of their economies and social structure, the author shows how vulnerable these towns were to the dismantling of the royal and ecclesiastical institutions that had provided considerable employment and status to the local urban population. Added to old rivalries between municipal elites, the granting of civil equality to Protestants exacerbated economic and political competition and brought latent religious antagonism into the open. The series of laws emanating from Paris that culminated in the Civil Constitution of the Clergy in July, 1791, became explosive when the local "patriots" began to inventory the property of the monasteries and convents. The Catholic majority at Montauban now associated civil equality of Protestants with an attack on the monasteries. Worse, they associated both with the radicals at Paris, the local Jacobin clubs, and the Protestant-dominated militia.

Garrett shows how the antagonism was inflamed by the Patriotic press on one side and the Lenten sermons of the clergy on the other. The rhetoric recalled the Wars of Religion in the sixteenth century, with the "fanatics" confronting "polluters" in Montauban in 1790. Garrett is especially effective in showing the escalation of rhetoric — France "a vast Calvary" or Catholics about to "drown the Constitution and its defenders in torrents of blood." It would be difficult to determine which religious group was more "fanatic." Following upon a religious procession in the baroque style, the Catholics humiliated the Protestants at Montauban by forcing them to remove their cockades in front of the cathedral. After the Protestants regained control with the aid of coreligionists from Bordeaux, the local Jacobin club accused the Catholic party of being part of the "aristocratic plot" and held Montauban in tight control, minority though the Protestants were. Yet Garrett insists that when the Protestant elite repressed dissent, it was because of memories of the Reformation and not because there was any full-blown popular counterrevolution in the making in southwest France.

Roderick Phillips presents us with a quiet revolution that did not, perhaps could not, succeed: a major effort to alter family relations and attitudes by the law. The intentions — at least by our late twentieth-century standards of equality between spouses and siblings, and greater equality between parents and children — seem worthy, indeed compelling. Could the paterfamilias model of a millennium be replaced by a family authority that was limited and accountable, akin to a constitutional monarchy if not to a republic? There were a few successes.

One major change was equality of inheritance that not even the Napoleonic Code could turn back in law or in practice. But especially in the area of husband-wife relations there were no major shifts of popular attitude. As a result, the new family law remained largely unenforceable.

Selecting Rouen as his case study, Phillips shows how the removal of church jurisdiction over the family created enormous difficulties in a Catholic society. Civil marriage and divorce were legislated in late 1792, but neither lay officials nor parish priests were prepared for it. Was a civil contract sufficient to legitimize marriage and the rights of inheritance? Was the new *état civil* reliable? More important, local officials by intention or habit often refused to apply the new law, neglecting to pursue paternity suits or ordering wives to return to their husbands or failing to investigate cases of marital violence. Popular resistance to civil marriage at Rouen is clearly attested to by Phillips's statistics. Numbers can still be telling. Divorce, on the other hand, was more popular, at least in the urban areas where women had some opportunity for economic independence.

One of the more intriguing puzzles was the failure of the family courts, intended to be rapid and cheap and also to contain the intimate details of family disputes within the family or among close friends. Yet somehow the lawyers crept back in. More significant, these courts were simply not used. Phillips suggests that only the bourgeoisie, who established them, were champions of privacy and the isolated nuclear family, whereas the popular classes were much more community-oriented and accustomed to more open family relations. One wonders, however, if a more formal court with legal counsel was not better insurance of privacy than the family tribunal where the relatives might learn too much about potential inheritances. Phillips concludes that the revolutionaries may have misjudged the familial sentiments and economic necessities of the majority of Frenchmen *and* Frenchwomen. The ideal of "equality and harmony within families" still confronted the cultural constraints of an Old Regime.

Nancy Fitch takes us to the remote backwater of rural France where Joseph Fouché earned his spurs as a "representative on mission for the Republic" in 1793. Not unlike Colin Lucas's Claude Javogues in the Loire department, Fouché was a man of extraordinary energy and dedication to the political education of the "People" in the abstract.[3] Hypnotized, it seems, by the Parisian revolutionary rhetoric, Fouché was ultimately unable to adapt the will of his People to the human beings of the towns and villages of the eastern Massif Central. Like Javogues, Fouché implemented the dechristianization policies from Paris with thoroughness and conviction, climaxing his campaign with the Festival of Brutus in the secularized cathedral in Nevers. But, writes Fitch, "unlike Furet, the historian, Fouché recognized the ambiguity inherent in this situation" where words and symbols replaced institutions as vehicles of power.

Fitch concludes that there was more than one political culture, and many dialogues took place between Paris and the provinces. She also relates Fouché's political language and policies to the social and economic structure of the Allier and Nièvre departments. Following Richard Cobb, Fitch claims the local Terror never ceased to resemble class warfare against the bourgeoisie and the village messieurs, especially the *gros fermiers*.[4] Ambiguities arose when even egalitarian Montagnards like Fouché had to face the sacred right of private property and to decide whether to appeal to the sharecroppers by giving them title to the land they worked. Were sharecroppers producers or consumers? Were they closer to wage laborers or to small capitalist farmers? How would they react to the Maximum? In any case, the revolutionary leadership in Paris would tolerate neither "anarchists" nor "*partageurs*" (dividers) of the land. Like leaseholders throughout France, the mass of sharecroppers gained little materially from the Revolution.

Donald Sutherland's overview of the Revolution in the provinces is a fitting conclusion to this collection. Sutherland begins by reviewing recent trends in the interpretation of the French Revolution, stressing how much of the new emphasis on political culture turns out to be the culture of an elite with little place for "the culture of ordinary people even in Paris, let alone the forgotten provinces." Yet he insists that all major crises of the Revolution occurred in the provinces. The radicalization of the Revolution must be understood in light of the provinces' response to concrete Parisian policies and not as the result of a self-generating ideology, Manichean or Rousseauian. Among these policies, the Civil Constitution of the Clergy caused the greatest and most unexpected resistance. One must descend from the olympian rhetoric of the Paris assemblies to the provincial police files in order to reconstruct a popular mentality that revolved about notions of community, liturgy, purity, and humanity. And to understand these words the historian must link this discourse to social structure, cultural traits, and political events in movement.

Sutherland defends this proposition by drawing upon his own research in Brittany as well as on Timothy Tackett's recent work on the ecclesiastical oath.[5] Successively, he investigates local conceptions of the priesthood, religiosity, leaseholding, population pressure, and the rise of rents and taxes, all of which combined to create disillusion and eventually hatred of the outsiders and their baggage of new phrases — "law," "citizen," "nation," "regeneration." Conscription was only the match to the combustible pile in the Vendée. Sutherland claims that his model, with its emphasis on the structure of landholding, works well for other (though not all) regions of France. He also stresses that the almost hysterical fear of counterrevolution caused the revolutionary government in Paris to enforce a drastic repression, especially of refractory priests, whom it stigmatized as the agents of counterrevolution. This was overreaction surely, but the provinces harbored real enemies of the Revolution just as surely.

Sutherland demonstrates how each successive crisis, far from rallying the nation, enlarged its circle of enemies, increased the ferocity of the repression, and spawned a civic education to "offset the odious influence of religion." The continued power of popular religion in the provinces revealed how alien the principles of 1789 were to many French peasants. The subtitle of Sutherland's article, "Class or Counterrevolution" might well read: "The Conflict of Two Irreconcilable Cultures." Complex indeed was the interaction of national politics and provincial tensions.

NOTES

1. Louis Bergeron and Jean Mayaud, *Histoire provinciale de la Révolution française* (Paris, 1988–) is a multivolume collection in process; Colin Lucas, ed., *The Documentary History of the French Revolution* (Oxford: Pergamon Press, 1990–) also a multivolume series, devotes ample space to the Revolution outside Paris and even outside France. See also Colin Lucas and Gwynne Lewis, *Beyond the Terror: Essays in French Regional and Social History, 1794–1800* (Cambridge, 1983); Donald Sutherland, *France, 1789–1815: Revolution and Counterrevolution* (Oxford, 1985), especially Sutherland's bibliographical essay on the Revolution in the provinces; Michel Vovelle, *The Fall of the French Monarchy, 1787–1792*, trans. Susan Burke (Cambridge, 1984);

Vovelle, *La Mentalité révolutionnaire* (Paris, 1986), *La Révolution française: Images et récits* (Paris, 1989), and *La Révolution contre l'église: De la Raison à l'Etre Suprême* (Paris, 1988).

2. François Furet, *Interpreting the French Revolution*, trans. Elborg Forster (Cambridge, 1981); F. Furet and Mona Ozouf, *Dictionnaire Critique de la Révolution française* (Paris, 1986); M. Ozouf, *Festivals and the French Revolution*, trans. Alan Sheridan (Cambridge, Mass., 1988); *L'Homme régénéré: Essais sur la Révolution française* (Paris, 1989); Maurice Agulhon, *Marianne into Battle: Republican Images and Symbolism in France, 1789–1880*, trans. Janet Lloyd (Cambridge, 1981); Lynn Hunt, *Politics, Culture, and Class in the French Revolution* (Berkeley, 1984); Robert Darnton and Daniel Roche, eds., *Revolution in Print: The Press in France, 1775–1800* (Berkeley, 1989); Keith Michael Baker and Colin Lucas, eds., *The French Revolution and the Creation of Modern Political Culture* (Oxford, 1987, 1989), 2 vols.; K. Baker, ed., *Inventing the French Revolution: Essays on French Political Culture in the 18th Century* (Cambridge and New York, 1990); Jack R. Censer, ed., *The French Revolution and Intellectual History* (Chicago, 1989).

3. Colin Lucas, *The Structure of the Terror: The Example of Javogues and the Loire* (Oxford, 1973).

4. Richard Cobb, *The People's Armies*, trans. Marianne Elliott (New Haven, 1987).

5. Timothy Tackett, *Religion, Revolution, and Regional Culture in Eighteenth-Century France: The Ecclesiastical Oath of 1791* (Princeton, 1986).

STEVEN G. REINHARDT

The Revolution in the Countryside: Peasant Unrest in the Périgord, 1789-90

ON MARCH 15, 1790, an alarmed official named André wrote to the authorities to denounce the people of his parish, Condat-sur-Vézère. Asking not to be identified for fear of reprisal, he described how one hundred peasants went to the local château in January, 1790. In the words of André, once the crowd arrived at the château, they

> . . . first stole all of the fish in the moat, then went inside and stole grain belonging to the seigneur's agent. They then took the grain measures used to collect seigneurial dues and burned them in public. From there they went to tear down the walls that enclosed a field of flax belonging to the seigneur and took possession of it. They pulled up the gallows and threw it into the river. Finally, they went into the parish church of Condat and removed all the church pews found therein, carried them to the square, and burned them in public. They explicitly warned the owners never to replace them in the future. Such is the conduct of the people of Condat, which, in these events, is quite reprehensible.

André went on to request that the authorities send someone to Condat to begin an investigation.[1] This incident was one of a number of disorders that also caused the Marquis Foucauld de Lardimalie, noble delegate of the second estate from the Périgord, to report to the Constituent Assembly in Paris, "My province is in flames. People without property are plundering those who do own property."[2]

A wave of peasant unrest swept across the province in the winter of 1789-90, with the most serious disorders occurring in the district known as the Sarladais. In sharp contrast to the marquis's exaggerated account, the province definitely was not in flames. In fact, the Périgourdin disorders seem remarkably tame. As seen in the parish of Condat, the violence involved in these incidents was rarely wanton and often targeted only symbols of privilege. Little significant damage was actually inflicted on people or property. Particularly from the vantage point of the twentieth century, the controlled violence engaged in by Périgourdin peasants seems bizarre, even quaint. I will argue that their actions can only be understood when viewed in light of the traditional forms of collective violence that had characterized peasant rebellions since at least the seventeenth century. Unsurprisingly, peasants who engaged in collective action during the winter and spring of 1789–90 expressed their discontent in a familiar idiom; yet they simultaneously adapted their traditional rites of violence to fit the new political situation.[3]

Occurring in an area that had remained relatively calm during the Great Fear of summer, 1789, the disorders in the Périgord were part of the peasant unrest that took place in more than three hundred parishes and affected nearly one hundred châteaux in the southwest between December, 1789, and March, 1790. Tensions had been mounting in this region during the final decades of the Old Regime due in large part to the oppressive weight of the seigneurial system.[4] Seigneurialism may have made some sense during the Middle Ages, when nobles had actually provided protection in exchange for the goods and services rendered by their serfs, yet by the end of the eighteenth century it was clearly anachronistic and served only to squeeze additional agricultural surplus out of an already hard-pressed peasantry. Although forms of personal servitude were rare in the southwest, harvest dues in the region were among the highest in the kingdom. To make matters worse, seigneurs were intensifying their pressure on the peasantry by reviving lapsed dues, revising estate registers and, in general, managing their estates more efficiently. The result was popular resentment of seigneurialism and the society of privileges that reinforced it.[5]

The unrest was also part of a wider wave of disturbances triggered by the Constituent Assembly's incomplete and conditional abolition of seigneurialism on August 4, 1789.[6] On that night, delegates who were alarmed by peasant rebellions across France found themselves caught up in what one delegate called a "contagion of sentimental feeling." They therefore voted to abolish the seigneurial regime in its entirety. In the cold light of subsequent days, however, they reconsidered and clarified their intentions. To the peasants it seemed contradictory to declare seigneurialism abolished and, at the same time, require peasants to continue paying their dues. Yet that is exactly what the assembly did in its proclamation of August 10, which sternly ordered peasants to pay their dues until compensation could be arranged for seigneurs.[7]

When autumn arrived in the southwest, it brought with it the normal contingent of seigneurs, landlords, and tithe collectors who turned up to collect their portion of the harvest. This time, however, peasants who had heard reports of the legislation passed between August 4 and 11 were determined to delay, reduce, or even refuse payment. In effect, they seized the initiative from the assembly sitting in Paris. From the day peasants saw the seigneurial regime survive despite its abolition in theory, they took it on themselves to deliver the final blow.[8]

The agrarian violence that erupted in the Périgord was therefore more than a blind panic or a descent into anarchy; it was purposeful in its goals and bore witness to the year-long politicization of the peasantry. Moreover, because bourgeois penetration into the seigneurial regime was pronounced in the district, the disorders targeted not only properties belonging to nobles but also those that had been purchased by members of the middle class. Whereas bourgeois proprietors were generally content to watch peasants attack seigneurialism, they were alarmed when their own private property was threatened. They therefore formed urban militias (forerunners of the National Guard) to repress peasant violence. As the unrest spread, frightened families from both social groups sought refuge in the towns and called on the royal mounted police (*maréchaussée*) to restore order.[9]

Given the overwhelmingly agricultural character of the Périgord, only a very small fraction of the inhabitants of small towns and *bourgs* did not participate in working the fields.[10] Village blacksmiths and weavers as well as small proprietors, sharecroppers, and landless workers can all safely be considered as part of the peasantry, which can be defined as "that portion of the population engaged in agricultural pursuits and who, by virtue of their close links to the soil, shared a common lifestyle and a common outlook."[11] Considered in this broad sense, the disorders of 1789–90 were undeniably peasant in origin and execution. Analysis of records on the individuals apprehended reveals that in the entire group, peasant proprietors (*laboureurs*) constituted approximately one quarter of the accused; sharecroppers, agricultural workers, and village artisans were also well represented. Equally significant is the fact that the rebels were predominantly young men:

sixty percent of those arrested were between twenty and thirty-four years of age.[12]

The unrest began in the countryside. The first major incident occurred in the parish of Paulin, at the château of the nobleman Joseph de Bar, seigneur de La Faurie. During the preceding years, de Bar apparently had alienated local peasants, who nursed longstanding grievances against him. When, in September, 1789, young men asked him to make a contribution to help celebrate the creation of the village militia, he refused and reprimanded them for carrying arms to divine services. The men replied with obscene insults. Later the seigneur begrudgingly made a small contribution, but in October peasants who gathered at the local fair were still criticizing the seigneur for his arrogance.[13]

On the evening of November 29, approximately fifteen peasants responded to a drummer's call to arms and marched to the gate of the château. Their leader, an agricultural worker (*travailleur*) named Jean Faucher, reportedly said that "there were no more gentlemen and that he would be sure to make the Sieur Debar dance."[14] He later explained that rumors were circulating in the area "that the Sieur Debar had to be arrested and brought to justice in Paris because he had committed crimes against the people."[15] No one responded to their knocks, so they forced the gate and entered the inner courtyard. When a shot was fired from the château, the angry invaders retreated to the outer courtyard, where they broke into the cellar and removed barrels and lumber to build a fire. The glow of the flames attracted neighbors, who gathered to dance by the light of the bonfire. Around midnight, a sort of truce was called; the seigneur, as a token of good will, sent out food and wine.

By daybreak, the outer court of the château was filled with more than two hundred people. Responding to the crowd's threats, de Bar finally asked the vicar of Paulin to act as mediator and receive the claims of the participants. The greatest number of demands called for the abandonment of seigneurial dues, the restitution of fines imposed by seigneurial courts, and the return of confiscated firearms, which peasants could not legally possess. De Bar agreed to all of the conditions and provided the claimants with written receipts and assurances, hard cash for smaller amounts, and I.O.U.s for larger amounts. These latter arrangements suggest a certain amount of discussion, bargaining, and consent.[16] Encouraged by their success, the peasants made similar demands at other châteaux and at the homes of curés. De Bar, recovered from his initial surprise, denounced them to the provost of the royal mounted police, who opened an inquest that resulted in the arrest of three peasants.[17]

Their incarceration in the royal prison at Sarlat caused a violent reaction. On the night of January 14–15, 1790, church bells sounded in eleven parishes, summoning some four to five thousand peasants to assemble at Salignac. There, they seized de Bar's nephew and confined him in the municipal prison. Having decided against hanging him, an armed band of two thousand bound him like a common criminal and led him off to Sarlat with a rope around his neck, treating him harshly along the way. It seems that everyone wanted to deliver a blow and pull off a piece of his clothing as a souvenir. The crowd marched straight to the royal prison in Sarlat, where they forced the jailer to imprison the nephew. They also called for the release of the three prisoners, threatening "fire and blood" if their demands were not met. Their threats were unnecessary. The newly elected municipal authorities of Sarlat had decided not to resist the invaders; instead, they met the crowd at the city gates and ordered the jailer to release the captives, who were led home in triumph. No damage to property or persons was reported in Sarlat.[18]

A few days later, on January 25, 1790, approximately three hundred armed peasants in the parish of Lachapelle-Péchaud went at nightfall to the nearby château of the seigneur Mirandol, where they forced him to provide food and drink. Half-drunk, many of them then surrounded, menaced, and insulted him. Although the incident was over in a few hours, it and the events at the château de La Faurie frightened bourgeois and nobles in the vicinity, almost all of whom retreated to Sarlat with their families.[19]

A second series of incidents was initiated on January 24, 1790, when a band of peasants obliged their local seigneur (de Lasserre) to give them one of the weathervanes from his château (at Molières). They then persuaded the seigneur to pay their expenses at the local tavern, where they went to eat and drink their fill. The group was led by a master mason, Jean Barbezieu (called Jardel), who also directed the removal of church pews. Under the Old Regime, only nobles were entitled to keep pews in the parish church; commoners had to stand during divine services.[20] In light of revolutionary declarations of equality, the continued possession of a pew was seen as an affront. The next day, the ringing of the parish church bell summoned two hundred peasants to gather in the village square to plant a maypole. Armed with guns and led by a man playing bagpipes, they set off for the nearby château of Masnègre to search for a weathervane to surmount their maypole.[21]

The sound of bagpipes soon could be heard at the château. The entire Masnègre family (the chevalier and his wife, two sons, a daughter-in-law and children) went out to meet the procession. Greetings were exchanged, but the meeting was formal, even hostile; the seigneur and his family were making the best of a bad situation. When the chevalier de Masnègre asked why they had come, they said they wanted "one of the weathervanes to place on top of a tree that they wished to plant," as well as wine, bread, and other food. The family agreed to provide these, but only if the banquet would be held at the local tavern. As for the weathervane, the chevalier offered them any or all of those on the château. A peasant climbed onto the roof and removed one.

But the seigneur and the peasants could not agree on the site of the banquet. The peasants insisted on eating in the château. The seigneur finally agreed to let them eat in the courtyard, where tables were set up, and he and his family personally served food and drink to the crowd. The peasants were convinced, however, that the château concealed a much-hated nobleman from the area. They insisted on searching the château, so the majority of them, led by Jardel, went inside. Jardel later testified that Madame de Masnègre offered him white bread and a bottle of wine and, drawing him aside, said, "My poor Jardel, eat and drink, but take care that no one harms me or M. de Masnègre." Jardel reassured her they would not be harmed and went outside to tell the others; he said it was enough to have frightened them.[22] The crowd was clearly more concerned with finding the fugitive nobleman than with harming the family. They searched the château in vain: one or two rooms were broken into, shutters were torn from windows, and fruit and vegetables drying in the attic were trampled underfoot. They also took three hunting guns, but did so openly and, in their own eyes, "justly."[23]

The disappointed crowd killed pigeons and poultry and then began to leave. The seigneur — along with his wife and children — accompanied them to the end of the lane. All danger seemed to have passed, until Jardel asked the noble to embrace him "since they were now all equal." The seigneur balked, refused the fraternal embrace, and only held out his hand. Several peasants then aimed their guns at him, and two or three insisted that Madame de Masnègre embrace them. She agreed and did so with disarming good grace. The next day, January 25, the crowd planted maypoles in the nearby villages of Thonac and Sergeac.[24]

In Thonac, tragedy was only narrowly averted. The curé had agreed to contribute bread and wine, but the jostling crowd invaded his wine cellar, attic, and kitchen to help themselves. Although the leaders of the crowd tried to control people, a hungry peasant helped himself to a pot simmering by the fire. When the curé tried to chase him away, the man struck the curé. Another aimed his gun at the curé, and someone else threatened to hit the curé with a bottle and hang him from the nearest tree. Cooler heads finally prevailed. In contrast, though, orderly peasants paid a visit to the curé of Sergeac, who wined and dined sixty persons in the local tavern without their doing the slightest damage.[25]

The unrest in the countryside did not go unnoticed in the towns. All of the above occurred just outside the small town of Montignac, which was divided between a newly formed "patriotic" committee and a more conservative party. Jean Périer, master carpenter, was a sincere and enterprising democrat who was initially a member of the patriotic committee but who soon proved too radical even for the patriots. In one of their meetings, he apparently demanded in a loud voice a reduced tax on bread and meat, as in Paris. This proposal very much pleased the common people but strongly displeased his colleagues. The *maréchaussée* intervened, but Périer's supporters prevented his arrest. He abandoned the patriotic party and even flirted with the opposition; when unrest erupted in the countryside, the carpenter sided with the peasants.[26]

Périer and his supporters reinforced the antiseigneurial movement under way in rural parishes by exacting contributions from local notables. The groups followed the customary rules and methods that characterized innumerable such levies in the southwest, but there were a few differences. The group not only gathered contributions for cele-

brations but also required in many houses restitutions of money in reparation of past injustices, thus adding a revolutionary dimension to the
traditional custom. These were not disorderly throngs at the doors of
clergy, nobles, and bourgeois. They were disciplined detachments (some
of them armed) that conducted themselves peacefully. Restitutions
were apparently collected with a certain amount of bargaining and
compromise. Moreover, Périer, who had been honored with the name
"Necker" by his followers, made every effort to keep the contributions
to a minimum.[27]

In the words of the historian Georges Bussière, "Périer raised the
jacquerie to the level of an institution."[28] The band deposited all receipts into a common purse that it placed in the hands of a treasurer
who settled debts with cabarets where the group ate and drank by
sending money orders signed "Neker de Périer." The fund even provided restitution for contributions that Périer and his followers felt had
been unjustly collected. On January 29, about eight hundred peasants
marched into Montignac behind Périer, who directed the crowd towards
the old château that dominated the town. Pointing towards the citadel,
he called on them to remove the weathervane from the roof. It was
done, but not without some difficulty. Given the fact that in the
southwest only a seigneur was entitled to place a weathervane on his
roof, its removal symbolically decapitated the power of high justice
in one fell swoop.[29]

Périer was now acting like master of the town. How would the
patriotic committee react? Périer and his men were even patrolling
the town to maintain order at night and to prevent attacks on private
property. At least one of the "patriots" counseled cooperation and provided a tree for their maypole as well as the oxen needed to transport
it. Périer, however, advised against planting the maypole and secretly
cut it into pieces before it could be raised. His moderation did little
to calm the fears of the patriots. Several of them decided to teach Périer
a lesson; on March 1, they not only assaulted and beat him but also
threatened to hang him, but him into pieces, and throw him off the
bridge.[30]

The antiseigneurial movement swept across the Sarladais, express-
ing itself most often in attacks on symbols of privilege and in the
planting of maypoles. In the parish of Paunat, for example, peasants
demonstrated their new spirit of equality by attacking church pews,

especially those belonging to seigneurial judges and prosecutors. Since the right to exercise justice had been abolished along with the rest of the seigneurial regime, peasants questioned why officials should retain these marks of their former authority. The curé described what happened in the following words: "The church bell sounded for four days, the parish rose up in arms to burn church pews and chairs, to eat and drink in the better homes, and to plant a maypole showing the abolition of seigneurial dues. Such were the tumultuous and scandalous scenes that afflicted us in the first few days of last February."[31] At the first rumor of trouble, two notables, Ducluzeau and Labrousse, removed their pews. Shortly afterwards, more than one hundred men armed with guns, hatchets, and batons entered the church and destroyed the pews and chairs found inside. They then burned the pieces in the public square. Overall, there was no violence, only eating and drinking at the expense of those who had had pews in the church.[32]

Frustrated that the pews of the above two had escaped their justice, peasants went to the home of Labrousse and tried to seize his pew. When Labrousse resisted, violence was only narrowly avoided. During the next three days, peasants complained about seigneurial dues, abuses in collection, and unjust legal actions. They continually made reference to the pews, these emblems of inequality that had escaped their leveling. On February 1, Ducluzeau submitted to popular pressure: he finally surrendered his pew and agreed to wine and dine the crowd. Moreover, he agreed under pressure to accompany the troop of about sixty as it made its rounds to the homes of other notables.[33]

Labrousse, however, refused to acknowledge the peasants' prerogatives. The inhabitants of the parishes of Paunat and Limeuil therefore invaded his home, demanded bread and wine, and would have raided his wine cellar if Ducluzeau had not intervened. When they asked Labrousse for his church pew, he told them he had burned it. The crowd therefore demanded and received planks of wood in its place. After stopping by other houses, the troop went to the public square, where they piled the pews, chairs, and planks for a bonfire. They also planted a maypole, on the top of which they attached symbols of seigneurial dues: grain measures and a chicken. Having lit the fire, several persons insisted that they burn the mill used to sift grain for payment of harvest dues. They were satisfied only when Ducluzeau gave them his own.[34]

Here, as elsewhere in France, the peasants displayed a fundamental if naive confidence in the monarchy. The fact that the peasant leader in the parish of Paunat was named "Rey," which in patois means "king" (*roi*), may have reinforced this deeply rooted tradition. Rey apparently was better off than most peasants and had great influence over his followers. When several of the more prosperous and respectable citizens of the parish came to ask Rey to stop the unrest, he invited them to dinner but refused to use his influence. Peasants in neighboring districts expressed the same confidence that their actions were royally sanctioned. In Quercy, it was said that the king, wearing wooden shoes (*sabots*) and peasant clothing, had shown up at church in the pew of a seigneur, who had shamelessly chased him away. That was why, peasants believed, the king had ordered all his subjects of the Third Estate to burn the pews.[35] Within the Périgord, the curé of Orliaguet reported that his parishioners erected a maypole, but he also explained that "the sign 'Vive le roy, Vive la nation' demonstrates very well that they did not plant a maypole in a spirit of revolt."[36] When later ordered to take down their maypoles, peasants said they would do so only after they had received express orders from the king.[37]

Peasants in the parish of Cendrieux, like those in Paunat, challenged the community's traditional elites, both noble and non-noble.[38] There the movement was led by the cabaret owner Louis Chantal and his younger brother Joseph, a merchant. As a result, the town had two militias: one commanded by a gentleman and one commanded by the cabaret owner. On January 31, the latter arrived in the public square with a drummer and twelve militiamen. He ordered the removal and public burning of all the church pews as well as the balustrade surrounding a chapel reserved for privileged persons. The next day they erected a maypole that bore a sign forbidding the payment of seigneurial dues.[39]

The leaders of the popular movement insisted on the legitimacy of their actions. One of the victims complained to the sister of the Chantal brothers; she replied that the same was being done in all the parishes by order of the king! The brothers later argued that the maypole was planted in the presence of the majority of the inhabitants and that several municipal officers and notables helped. The same was true of church pews, they said, which were burned with the consent of the owners, who were present at the event, and with the permission of the mayor. They emphasized that there were no forced contributions and that Louis Chantal himself had thrown the first *louis* into the basket that served as collection box.[40]

In the nearby parish of Salon, we again find the belief that orders came from the king. On February 2, the commander of the militia stood in front of the church after mass to read the letters patent for the formation of the municipality. Since he also served as agent for the seigneur, his listeners were understandably suspicious. When he insisted that they must not imitate people in neighboring parishes who had burned church pews, the crowd grew impatient. They accused the commander of trying to thwart the orders of the king and of "having hidden these orders from them and having read only the ones he wished to read."[41] One of the leaders, named Négroux, approached a bourgeois, touched him on the breeches, and said: "Your breeches are not dirty, like mine." He added, addressing the commander, "There is not enough room in the church; it is your fault if there is not enough room for stools for us. If there were, I would not have dirtied my breeches and stockings."[42] Several persons then called for burning the pews of the privileged and the erection of a maypole. They insisted that the commander of the militia direct the operation, but he refused. They then tried to make a bailiff lead them, but he also refused. So they finally forced the beadle to tell everyone "to come to Mass the next day and that they would drink a pint and amuse themselves." The next day, fifty peasants led by Négroux and the sharecropper Mandrin seized church pews, starting with that of the commander.[43]

Regardless of the region, peasants impelled by an indigenous sense of popular justice bestowed upon their actions a lawful and quasi-official character. Moreover, they did not doubt that the king, whom they believed had their best interests at heart, truly intended to right the wrongs they suffered. Why else, they reasoned, would he have invited them to draw up their list of grievances in the spring of 1789? Because their conduct appeared legitimate to them, they believed it surely must be sanctioned by the king.[44]

Property owners understandably did not share this point of view and called for repression. In Paris, representatives from Périgord, Quercy, Rouergue, and Limousin made desperate appeals to the Constituent Assembly. Locally, the newly formed municipal governments and their militias began to take measures against these movements.

In Sarlat, bourgeois formed a National Guard because, as they stated, "on all sides the only thing one hears talked about are seditious gatherings and brigandage, and the most honest inhabitants of the countryside are fearful not only for their property but also for their lives." Proof that their fears were not groundless, they said, was the fact that Jardel, leader of the action at Masnègre, had been captured in Sarlat itself, where he had come to "exact contributions."[45]

Jardel was either very brave or very foolhardy in trying to recover three guns confiscated from his father by a nobleman. What is more likely is that he firmly believed he was acting legitimately. Jardel was proud of his role in the action at Masnègre and, in the words of one observer, "believed that what he was doing was the most natural thing in the world."[46] He had already approached the late nobleman's eldest son, who surrendered a gun without protest. So Jardel went to Sarlat on market day, only five days after the incident at Masnègre, with the intention of recovering two more guns, one from each of the nobleman's daughters. When bystanders heard him say that he would recover his guns or someone would pay, his ambiguous remark was construed as a menace. He was arrested and led off to prison. On February 17, other participants in the incident at Masnègre joined Jardel in captivity.[47]

In response to the appeal of local authorities, the provost general of Guyenne, Pierre Barthélemy Revoux de Ronchamp, came to Sarlat, where he was joined by his lieutenant from Périgueux, Louis Bovier de Bellevaux. They ordered brigades of the *maréchaussée* from the surrounding districts to gather at Sarlat. A detachment of the Royal-Polish regiment arrived from Cahors and began making arrests. Towns such as Terrasson and Belvès organized their own militias to maintain order.[48] The latter sent its militia against peasants in the vicinity of Cabans who had burned church pews and forbidden the payment of seigneurial dues. The leader, Géraud Laval (called Repayré), felt he had little to fear since he had used no violence; he therefore allowed himself to be captured without resistance. The militia arrested two others, Jean Soustre and Hugon (called Quinquayré), and turned them over to the provost court (*prévôté*) in Sarlat.

Rebellious peasants began to fill Sarlat's prison, but due, perhaps, to fear of what the future might bring, no one took the initiative to judge or condemn them. The provost court finally convicted Repayré of destroying church pews, obstructing the collection of seigneurial dues, and using armed force to exact contributions. He was condemned to be hanged in the public square; some of his accomplices were sentenced to serve five years in the galleys, others only one year. The sentences, however, were never carried out. On March 7, the Constituent Assembly decided to minimize further bloodshed and so granted a reprieve to the accused.[49]

Official repression was, on the whole, ambivalent and relatively mild. The electoral chamber of Sarlat, which acted as a kind of patriotic committee, had called for help from the National Assembly. Yet, the chamber also showed a certain indulgence towards the uprisings. The author of the February 3, 1790, address to the assembly wrote: "The suffering that such widespread disorders caused is attenuated when we reflect that in the midst of the license these unhappy people were not ferocious. There were no murders, and if they were capable of several profanations, it was never anything to make nature blush. Moreover, the people were tricked by the false edicts and false decrees of the National Assembly."[50] By that date, the crisis had passed and calm was returning. Yet not everyone was satisfied. In the debates before the Constituent Assembly, Foucauld de Lardimalie, who was a grand seigneur and recipient of revenues valued at six hundred thousand livres, complained that he would have difficulty collecting them. Maximilien de Robespierre intervened in the heated discussions. He judged the use of force imprudent "against people accused of burning châteaux" and refused to refer to them as brigands, despite protests from Foucauld.[51]

In general, the provost court resisted the pressure of conservatives and took little action. Popular resistance and the rapid march of events prevented the pursuit of inquests; if the mounted police did arrest culprits, they usually released them several days later.[52] No one was actually executed in the Périgord. The grand provost of Guyenne did call on all curés to exhort their parishioners to take down the maypoles, these "monuments of insurrection," that had been erected in nearly every parish.[53] Although most localities reluctantly complied, several showed unexpected resistance.

Distrustful peasants in the parishes of Sainte-Nathalène and Prats-de-Carlux said they would obey only when they were shown the written order of the king. The curé of Prats observed: "Unfortunately, however, we are no longer listened to and they have almost no confidence in us."[54] The curé of Couze-de-Saint-Front wrote to the provost about his rebellious parishioners in the following terms: "They do not trust me and are themselves persuaded and can see that the order did not come from the king but from the nobility and clergy who, they believe, bear them ill will. They are now saying that I gave you 40 livres to obtain the order to take down the maypole they planted. If I read the order, they will be even more ill-disposed towards me."[55]

Peasants were irritated and offended by the clergy's support for the dismantling of their "monuments." The consequences for curés ranged from the comic to the tragic. The congregation of Mauxens-de-Miremont had its revenge by voting to dismiss the bell ringer the curé had chosen two years before and replacing him with the village drunkard. Much more seriously, the curé of Rouchard — when called before the revolutionary tribunal during the Terror to answer other charges — found he was bitterly reproached for his earlier support of the seigneurs, his opposition to the maypole, and his denunciation of four parishioners. He was condemned to death.[56]

One curé asked the bishop whether he should refuse the sacraments to participants in the disorders and make them either return goods or pay compensation to the victims of requisitions. The curé of Villac acted independently without asking for instructions. His parishioners had planted a maypole and enjoyed the food and drink "contributed" by the richest taxpayers. Although such contributions were not always made without reservations, the two donors in this case had shown little reluctance. The curé of Villac nonetheless construed the peasants' actions as sinful if not sacrilegious. As Easter approached, he announced during mass that all those who had eaten and drunk at the expense of the donors had to provide restitution or he would refuse to hear their confessions. Some parishioners agreed to do so, but others refused. The curé apparently kept his word and denied the sacraments to anyone who failed to obey.[57]

In contrast, many curés were quick to defend their parishioners, insisting that they had done nothing wrong and that the erection of maypoles should not be seen as seditious. Some few curés enjoyed the support of their parishioners and actually headed disorders. On September 4, 1790, the electoral assembly of the department of the Dordogne, anxious to efface all reminders of the disorders of that spring, notified parishes that church pews could be replaced. When a notable in the parish of Calviac tried to replace his pew, the vicar prevented him and called on parishioners to block all future efforts. When municipal officials arrived at the church to investigate, about thirty angry persons threatened to "cut them in pieces and set fire to their houses" if they did not leave. The vicar was further accused of telling his parishioners it was permissible to destroy châteaux and "that they must divide up property and each person would have his share." Although the accusations reflect the paranoia of the authorities more than anything else, the fact remains that the vicar certainly enjoyed the confidence and support of his parishioners, who were extremely reluctant to abandon symbols of their equality and liberty.[58] Here as elsewhere, when the authorities attempted to remove symbols of peasant power, the threat of bloodshed often forced them to back down.[59]

To understand the significance of these disorders, we must place them within the context of the popular revolts that had shaken southwestern France in the early seventeenth century. In the Aquitaine, revolt was a cultural fact: the region was dangerous from the crown's point of view because of the long-standing character of the privileges enjoyed by its towns and provinces. This special immunity convinced its inhabitants of the legitimacy of their tax rebellions. Broad-based collective action and ritualized violence had long been the norm in these disturbances. In the summer of 1635, news of antifiscal riots in Bordeaux touched off a riot in Périgueux. The royal tax collectors took refuge in the city jail and were beseiged for two days. When they were finally captured, the crowd threw them into the Couderc well, a deep, polluted well usually kept covered. In fact, the uncovering of the well just before the riot began had been interpreted as a signal of the approaching sedition. The people were exerting their right to purge alien — in this case, royal — elements from their midst.[60]

That same month, fear of new taxes led to a kind of witch hunt (*chasse aux gabeleurs*) for royal fiscal agents in the city of Agen. This fear culminated in the beating to death of victims, the abuse and mutilation of their bodies, and the pillage and burning of their houses. The revolt lasted two days and left fifteen dead. The participants again were artisans and innkeepers, plus thousands of peasants who poured into the city. Everyone seems to have participated, including the municipal authorities (*consuls*), who were required to join the demonstrators. The murders were truly collective acts. One observer noted that "there wasn't a child or a good mother who did not give the corpse a blow with a stick or a kick."[61] Several bodies were mutilated, torn apart, and others stabbed dozens of times. Since these murders were seen as acts of justice, the victims were given a chance to confess and say their prayers before meeting their fate. Their homes were torn down and burned, their papers and books destroyed.

The uprisings that occurred in the Périgord between 1637 and 1641 are the most famous in French history because they involved the largest number of peasants (known as *Croquants*) and most nearly attained success. The uprisings began when the government announced an extraordinary military levy of grain; within one week a peasant army was on the march. On May 7–8, 1637, an assembly of at least thirty thousand peasants met and selected a force of eight thousand men who had previous military experience. On May 10, this army captured the town of Bergerac, and within three weeks the rebels were masters of the Périgord. The Croquants planned to march on Bordeaux, mobilizing the towns along the way, but no towns rallied to their cause. The revolt therefore remained rural in character. In late May they marched southward, into the Agenais. On June 1, a force of three thousand royal troops met the rebels in a pitched battle at the small town of La Sauvetat. House-to-house fighting ensued, with the royal troops setting fire to houses to drive out the rebels. The town was taken after bloody fighting that left between two hundred and eight hundred dead among the attackers and a thousand to fifteen hundred dead among the Croquants. When confronted with such decisive military force, the peasant forces melted away. Only forty prisoners were taken. The tradition of collective resistance would survive, however, and take decades to eradicate.[62]

We must also view the revolutionary disorders of 1789–90 within the context of the day-to-day violence that had occurred in the area during the preceding twenty years. The criminal court records of the Sénéchaussé of Sarlat, the royal court with jurisdiction over the southeastern portion of the Périgord, show that the rituals, language, and goals of the action taken by individuals and groups between 1770 and 1789 were at least superficially similar to those employed in the seventeenth century.[63] Villagers assembled by the ringing of the church bell or the beating of a drum seized their flails, *batons*, pitchforks, and stones, and threatened their enemies with ritual dismemberment and ceremonial ablution. Collective action retained certain aspects of carnival: music and dancing sometimes preceded or followed charivaris and mock battles between parish youths, and drummers and pipers often led crowds into action. The goal of collective violence was still the defense and restoration of communal solidarity via the chastisement (whether symbolic or actual) of the offender. When satirical sanctions such as charivaris elicited an admission of guilt and true penitence, the wayward son or daughter was readmitted to the social body. Significantly enough, however, large-scale insurrections were unknown in the region between 1770 and 1789.[64]

By the end of the eighteenth century, popular collective action in the Sarladais had changed in several respects. Most importantly, the disorders of the last twenty years of the Old Regime were no longer directed against royal fiscal agents. They were instead directed against persons actually residing in the rural world: landowners and seigneurs (or their agents) who were maximizing profits by collecting rents and seigneurial dues much more carefully. During the disturbances of 1790, the targets of revolt were seigneurs, curés, and rural bourgeois. Within that group, seigneurs were hit the hardest. Significantly, though, rural bourgeois who often acted as attorneys, notaries, fiscal agents, and judges for seigneurs were targets in thirty percent of the incidents.[65]

The greater degree of solidarity that formed the basis of the Croquants' large-scale violent resistance had progressively eroded in the course of the eighteenth century. The local community in a relatively backward area such as the Sarladais, although perhaps retaining a greater degree of solidarity than it did elsewhere in France, was nonetheless affected by this process. The theoretical bond of protection and allegiance between nobles and peasants continued to dissolve, if it had not disappeared entirely. Peasants increasingly saw nobles for what they had become: tax-exempt parasites who abused their traditional privileged position in society to maintain their economic advantage over the peasantry. During the Revolution, peasants once again rose in revolt, but this time the target was not the state, for which taxes seemed an unavoidable fact of existence. Instead, the target was the local château, which was controlled by a nobleman who had become estranged from the rural community.[66]

The destruction of the symbols of seigneurial power inaugurated

the revolutionary violence. The peasants attacked the "foremost in-
habitant of the parish" by attacking the symbols of his prerogatives:
the church pew and family tomb he held in the parish church and
especially the weathervanes that surmounted his château. In the southwest, possession of a weathervane was an honorific privilege restricted
to holders of fiefs. Investing customary rituals with new political content, peasants rejected anything that had the least air of distinction,
adopted new conduct, refused to lift their hats, omitted the particle
in the seigneur's name, and claimed a fraternal embrace. The leveling
was combined with jubilant provocation and even, in some places, a
tendency to "turn the world upside down," with peasants now on top.[67]

The attack was not limited to symbols of power, but also targeted
the more practical economic foundations of the seigneurie, such as
harvest dues and fisheries. In some areas, peasants drained lakes that
provided fish for aristocratic tables yet caused fogs and fevers. In many
places peasants took possession of the château, stripped it of consum-
ables, and pilfered small objects. But the real goal of such visits was
to make the seigneurs recognize the legitimacy of the peasants' actions.
They required the prompt return of titles, papers, and documents relative to agricultural rents, as well as receipts for payments in arrears,
and even the restitution of firearms and fines unjustly collected.[68]

After the war against symbols of authority and the temporary
seizure of châteaux, the peasants served public notice of the new bal-
ance of power. They therefore brought their actions to a climax with
the planting of maypoles, symbols of fertility and peasant potency that
crowned and culminated what had already taken place.[69] In certain
regions, especially the Limousin, the maypole traditionally served as
a rallying point on feast days. Folklorists distinguish between the blos-
soming tree branch or bouquet of flowers (*mai*) that young men placed
before the homes of young women in the month of May, and the larger
poles or trees (generally pines or poplars) planted collectively in the
middle of the village or market place.[70] Cutting and erecting such maypoles required the participation not just of young men but of the entire community.[71]

The tops of the maypoles (*maieroles*) of the Limousin were decorated with bouquets of spring flowers. A sentiment of joy always prevailed at the planting of these symbols of rejuvenation. The maypoles
of January, 1790, were also crowned with ribbons, laurel, bouquets

of flowers, and placards bearing patriotic inscriptions. The Revolution had come, so the maypole became revolutionary, transformed in character into an important symbol of promised deliverance. In a pointed yet nonviolent fashion, it recalled to seigneurs their abusive means of measuring and sifting the grain for seigneurial rents: from the maypole, peasants hung sieves, brooms, grain measures, and weathervanes, the supreme ornament to bring down the pride of the seigneur. One historian, Georges Bussière, refers to maypoles as the "cahiers" of the Fourth Estate of peasants.[72]

The mounted police sent from Périgueux to halt the erection of a maypole at Saint-Géral found that the inhabitants had planted in front of the church door a tall tree, its summit shaped into a gallows, from which hung various symbols of authority including a writing desk and quill pen, and a placard with the inscription "Final receipt for rents." The tree was surmounted by the weathervane of the local seigneur. This display recapitulated the revolt that had just taken place by demonstrating the peasants' appropriation of the former instruments of domination, including justice. The maypole had effectively supplanted the seigneurial gallows. The peasants thereby called into question everything they considered an abuse of power. The Vicomte de Noailles, in early February, 1790, described events to the Constituent Assembly in the following manner: "In the Rouergue, Limousin, and Périgord, there are persons who have set themselves up as repairers of wrongs; they judge anew cases judged over the last thirty years and render sentences that they then execute."[73]

With the planting of the maypole, peasants celebrated. Every revolt included a feast of bread and wine as well as rarer dishes prepared for special occasions. Such feasting began with tours of collection (*quêtes*) around the parish, as was traditionally done when a maypole was planted or during the Christmas or Easter season.[74] Because generosity, a sense of *noblesse oblige*, was one of the social qualities expected of the *notable*, the peasant troops made their way to the best houses of the parish, including that of the curé. Notables willing to contribute to seasonal collections perhaps sensed the new political content of the exactions of 1790, which were more or less compulsory, and feared they represented a challenge to property rights.[75] The danger had always existed that such collections, when confronted with resistance, could become forced contributions. Peasant participants in the exactions of 1790 targeted those who possessed church pews and then characterized their exactions as just compensation for establishing equality in the new nation.[76]

The rites of revolt also took advantage of the specific sociability of youth, which did not stop with the frontier of marriage. Youths and young adults between the ages of fifteen and thirty-five (notably artisans) constituted the great majority of revolt participants in 1789–90. The planting of a *mai* was one of the principal customs ordinarily practiced by unmarried young males, whom the community informally designated to regulate the integrity of its territory, the exchange of women and goods, and the enforcement of customary rights. Their actions had always possessed the potential to subvert authority and even turn violent. Village sociability therefore reinforced social structure to give to youths and artisans the foremost role in the revolutionary disorders.[77]

What is more, we must remember that the disorders of 1790 coincided with the carnival season, a time traditionally associated in the minds of peasants with the ritualized chastisement of transgressors and with a certain licentiousness. The carnival season was marked by the subversion of order, the suspension of the rules of normal life, the right to personal and collective reprimand and ridicule, and the emergence of sexual acts and symbols. The principle of of inversion prevailed during carnival, when masters and servants exchanged places, when death gave way to life. According to the Russian literary critic, Mikhail Bakhtin, "Carnival celebrated temporary liberation from the prevailing truth and from the established order; it marked the suspension of all hierarchical rank, privileges, norms, and prohibitions. Carnival was the true feast of time, the feast of becoming, change, and renewal."[78] During the carnival season, all were considered equal. In brief, carnival celebrated the temporary destruction of the old world and the birth of the new world, of the new year, the new spring, the new regime.[79] What better season could be found for the dismantling of the Old Regime and the destruction of its symbols of oppression?

The objectives of the collective violence made a wide consensus possible among the peasantry, but during these actions society as a whole was, in the words of Mona Ozouf, simultaneously "torn apart by confrontation and welded together by solidarity."[80] The disorders of 1789–90 neglected and even contested the traditional leaders of the community. These revolts had their origin in the antagonism felt between those who lived from the work of their own hands and those who lived off the work of others.[81] Moreover, the disorders that occurred were strangely attenuated versions of the peasant revolts of the previous century. Although a continuity of language, rituals, and goals is clearly evident, the level of intensity was obviously lower. Whereas seventeenth-century Croquants actually dismembered and mutilated their victims before throwing them into a well or river, eighteenth-century peasants only threatened to do so. The revolutionary disorders were directed primarily against symbols: peasants raised maypoles on which they figuratively executed symbols of seigneurial authority, and they forced nobles to shake hands and drink with them as a sign of their newfound equality. But the reports that arrived in Paris of a Périgord in flames were unfounded in reality.

By way of explanation, we must remember that standards of behavior were changing. Whereas all groups previously had tolerated higher levels of personal violence and had accepted collective violence as a feature of popular justice, members of the middle class were increasingly unwilling to do so. The communal solidarity on which that earlier consensus depended had been undermined by economic change.[82] Can we go one step further, though, and argue that the relative scarcity of serious violence in the Périgord meant that the region had finally become more "civilized"? Here we must be very cautious. We must remember that during the Revolution other, more economically advanced regions of France (notably the Midi-Toulousain) experienced violence which, in its abundance and brutality, equaled if it did not surpass the viciousness of that in earlier centuries.[83]

In part, the avoidance of loss of life in the Périgord may have been due as much to chance as anything. Any number of incidents could easily have turned ugly. Yet, the fact that violence was averted is, I believe, significant. Seigneurs and peasants, although increasingly alienated over economic affairs, at least still understood the same ritual gestures and symbolic language. If they had been separated by greater cultural distance, then the nature of their confrontation arguably would have been much more abrupt, even brutal. Had seigneurs refused to yield and denied the participants' claims to be acting legitimately, the results might very well have been much more violent.[84]

Finally, we must recognize that although peasants retained familiar forms of collective action, they modified the content of their rites and rhetoric to address the novel circumstances of the late eighteenth century. As a result, they were able to employ effective popular sanctions that stopped short of atavistic violence. In the summer of 1789 and again in the spring of 1790, peasants in the countryside seized the initiative from the bourgeois delegates in Paris and propelled the French Revolution beyond limits that had not been dreamed of only one year earlier. The cycle of peasant resistance to seigneurialism would escalate steadily over the next two years. Yet, the ultimate demise of the seigneurial regime would require the intervention of the Jacobin-led Convention, which voted on July 17, 1793, to abolish it unconditionally, without compensation.[85]

NOTES

Portions of this article have appeared in my piece "Ritual Violence in Eighteenth-Century Périgord," in *The French Revolution in Culture and Society*, ed. David G. Troyansky, Cismaru, and Norwood Andrews, Jr. (Westport, Conn., 1990).

1. Archives Nationales (hereafter cited as AN), D XXXIX, Dossier 73, Lettres de trente-cinq curés du Sarladais, Lettre No. 23 (15 mars 1790).

2. The Marquis Foucauld de Lardimalie appeared before the assembly on February 2, 1790. He was seconded by Loys, the deputy of Sarlat, and by representatives from Quercy, Rouergue, and Limousin. Georges Bussière, *Etudes historiques sur la révolution en Périgord* (Bordeaux, 1877–1903), III, 284. Also see René Pijassou, "La crise Révolutionnaire," in Arlette Higounet-Nadal, ed., *Histoire du Périgord* (Toulouse, 1983), 258.

3. See Jean Boutier, "Jacqueries en pays croquant: Les révoltes paysannes en Aquitaine (décembre 1789–mars 1790)," *Annales: Economies, sociétés, civilisation* 34 (1979): 760. For risings in other regions, see D. M. G. Sutherland, *France, 1789–1815: Revolution and Counterrevolution* (Oxford, 1985), 74–75. Also see Samuel F. Scott, "Problems of Law and Order during 1790, the 'Peaceful' Year of the French Revolution," *American Historical Review* 80 (1975): 859–88.

4. Tackett notes that the antiseigneurial uprisings of 1790 seemed to occur in areas previously unaffected by violence in 1789 and where seigneurial dues were heaviest and paid in kind. Timothy Tackett, *Religion, Revolution, and Regional Culture in Eighteenth-Century France: The Ecclesiastical Oath of 1791* (Princeton, 1986), 189.

5. Jones reports that "in the Southwest harvest dues seem to have been both exceedingly onerous and exceedingly extensive." (49) He further argues that the "seigneurial reaction" was very real albeit extended over a longer period than previously thought. P. M. Jones, *The Peasantry in the French Revolution* (Cambridge, 1988), 44–45, 48–49, 54–57. Also see Sutherland, *France, 1789–1815*, 70–73.

6. Although it was once thought that the antiseigneurial riots of 1790 broke out across the entire nation, research reveals that their incidence was restricted to 38 districts in 17 departments, out of a total of over 500 districts. Tackett, *Religion, Revolution, and Regional Culture*, 187.

7. Georges Lefebvre, *The Coming of the French Revolution* (Princeton, 1947), 162–68. The assembly considered harvest dues as part of an original contract between the lord as owner and the person to whom he ceded a holding; it therefore decreed their redemption at a rate (fixed on May 3, 1790) amounting to twenty times the money fee, twenty-five times the fee in kind. Georges Lefebvre, *The French Revolution*, vol. 1: *From Its Origins to 1793* (New York, 1962), 164.

8. Earlier disorders in the Périgord were minor in comparison to those of the winter of 1789–90. The Great Fear, which swept through the region on July 29–30, 1789, did not cause any major disturbances but did result in the creation in nearly every commune of National Guard units that played a significant role in later disorders. Georges Lefebvre, *The Great Fear: Rural Panic in Revolutionary France*, trans. Joan White (New York, 1973), 192–94. Also see Pijassou, "La crise Révolutionnaire," 258; Sutherland, *France, 1789–1815*, 101–03; and Jones, *The Peasantry in the French Revolution*, 70, 79–81, 85.

9. Boutier, "Jacqueries en pays croquant," 771–72. Bourgeois proprietors would play a highly ambiguous role in the disorders of 1789–90. Jones, *The Peasantry in the French Revolution*, 49–53.

10. The largest urban centers in the Sarladais were still relatively small. In the later eighteenth century, Sarlat had 5,250 inhabitants; Montignac had 3,053; Terrasson numbered 2,961; Domme/Cénac had 2,747; Belvès had 2,075, and Saint-Cyprien had 2,055. Anne-Marie Cocula, "Vivre et survivre en Périgord au XVIIIe siècle," in Higounet-Nadal, *Histoire du Périgord*, 210–11, 264; André de Fayolle, *Topographie agricole du département de la Dordogne en Fructidor an IX* (Périgueux, 1939), 16; Guillaume Delfau, *Annuaire statistique du département de la Dordogne pour l'an XII* (Périgueux, 1804), 55. Archives Departementales de la Dordogne (hereafter cited as ADD) 6 M 10: Recensement de population (1806).

11. Jones, *The Peasantry in the French Revolution*, 7.

12. In the southwest, many persons classified as *laboureurs* were, in fact, share-croppers. The figures for the Aquitaine as a whole are from Boutier, "Jacqueries en pays croquant," 771–72; Jones, *The Peasantry in the French Revolution*, 10–11, 74–77. Bussière also notes that in the Périgord the man who worked a specific piece of land was commonly referred to as "*laboureur.*" *Etudes historiques*, III, 238.

13. Jean-Joseph Escande, *Histoire de Sarlat* (Sarlat, 1903), 277–78.

14. Bussière, *Etudes historiques*, III, 245.

15. ADD B 3614: Interrogatoire de Faucher (3 janvier 1790).

16. The vicar convinced the seigneur to grant three restitutions of land, two re-imbursements of legal expenses, two returns of confiscated firearms, the cancelation of receipts for unpaid debts and arrears, and four reimbursements of arrears of rent already paid (two going back more than twenty years). ADD B 3614: Requis du procureur du roi (8 décembre 1789); Boutier, "Jacqueries en pays croquant," 763–64.

17. ADD B 3614, Maréchaussée: Affaire de sédition à la paroisse de Paulin, 1789. Also see Bussière, *Etudes historiques*, III, 247–48.

18. The badly shaken nephew was later released under the protection of the vicar general of the archdiocese. ADD B 3614: Procès-verbal (16 janvier 1790); Bussière, *Etudes historiques*, III, 250–52.

19. Escande, *Histoire de Sarlat*, 278–79.

20. The right to have a pew in the choir of the parish church was one of the honorific rights. Denis Diderot, ed., "Droits honorifiques," *Encyclopédie, ou diction-naire raisonnée des sciences, des arts et des métiers* (Paris, 1755), V, 142–43.

21. The incident took place in and around the parish of Valojoulx. ADD B 1688:

Continuation d'Information (8 février 1790). For a descriptive summary of the incident, see Escande, *Histoire de Sarlat*, 280–82.

22. The nobleman they were searching for was M. Fompitou de Massacré, seigneur de Saint-Geniès. ADD B 1688: Interrogatoire de Jean Barbezieu, dit Jardel (14 février 1790).

23. Bussière, *Etudes historiques*, III, 264–65.

24. Escande, *Histoire de Sarlat*, 281.

25. Bussière, *Etudes historiques*, III, 266–67.

26. Bussière, *Etudes historiques*, III, 269.

27. They called another leader "Lafayette." Bussière, *Etudes historiques*, III, 270.

28. Bussière, *Etudes historiques*, III, 270.

29. Bussière, *Etudes historiques*, III, 270–72.

30. Périer was rescued by his supporters and brought suit against his assailants. ADD B 1599: Plainte (3 mars 1790) and Information (6 mars 1790). Bussière, *Etudes historiques*, III, 273–74.

31. AN D XXXIX, Dossier 73, Lettre No. 26 (9 mars 1790).

32. The "honnêtes bourgeois" who made forced contributions later denounced four leaders to obtain justice and reparation. The plaintiffs finally accepted a settlement of 60 *livres* in exchange for dropping their complaint. AN D XXXIX, Dossier 73, Lettre No. 26 (9 mars 1790).

33. Bussière, *Etudes historiques*, III, 275–78.

34. Bussière, *Etudes historiques*, III, 278–79.

35. Boutier, "Jacquerie en pays croquants," 768.

36. AN D XXXIX, Dossier 73, Lettre No. 12 (9 mars 1790).

37. Bussière, *Etudes historiques*, III, 279–80.

38. The curé of Paunat reported that the municipality had not yet been formed there because the peasants wished to exclude all the *honnêtes bourgeois* whereas the latter wished to exclude the authors of the disorders. AN D XXXIX, Dossier 73, Lettre No. 26 (9 mars 1790).

39. Bussière, *Etudes historiques*, III, 280–81.

40. Ibid., 281–82.

41. Ibid., III, 283.

42. Ibid.

43. Ibid., III, 283–84.

44. For a discussion of the concept of popular justice, see my article, "The Selective Prosecution of Crime in Ancien Régime France: Theft in the Sénéchaussée of Sarlat," *European History Quarterly* 16 (1986): 11–12, 19–20. Also see Edward P. Thompson, "The Moral Economy of the English Crowd in the Eighteenth Century," *Past and Present* 50 (1971): 76–136. For the more general issue of peasant reactions to the drawing up of the *cahiers de doléances*, see Sutherland, *France, 1789–1815*, 59–60.

45. ADD B 1599: Procès-verbal (30 janvier 1790).

46. Bussière, *Etudes historiques*, III, 288.

47. The municipal tribunal declared itself incompetent in the affair and referred it to the prévôté of the *maréchaussée* (ADD B 1688; Bussière, *Etudes historiques*, III, 288–89).

48. AN D XXXIX, Dossier 73, Lettre No. 20 (8 mars 1790).

49. ADD B 1689: Lettres de dénonciation (3–5 février 1790); and B 1701: Sentence (13 avril 1790). The assembly granted a reprieve in order to avoid executions such as those that had taken place at Brives and Tulle. The assembly finally suspended the *prévôté*

on September 11, 1790. Bussière, *Etudes historiques*, III, 296–97, 322–24. Also see Escande, *Histoire de Sarlat*, 283.

50. The author was probably the curé Pontard, vicar of Sainte-Marie de Sarlat, a popular and liberal priest who later would become a member of the legislature and a constitutional bishop (Bussière, *Etudes historiques*, III, 251–52, 292).

51. Bussière, *Etudes historiques*, III, 292–93.

52. When complaints flooded the *prévôté* of the *maréchaussée*, court officers registered them, ordered an inquiry, sometimes interviewed a few witnesses, but never took the case further than the inquest. Only when the accused was literally handed over to them did the investigation proceed — only to end in the provisional release of the accused when tempers had cooled. Iain A. Cameron, *Crime and Repression in the Auvergne and the Guyenne, 1720–1790* (Cambridge, 1981), 252–53.

53. The grand provost, Revoux de Ronchamps, received letters from 35 curés who described the disorders in their parishes. These letters are found in AN D XXXIX, Dossier 73. Two representatives from the National Assembly reported that every village in the contiguous district of Gourdon had a maypole, and some even had two or three (Bussière, *Etudes historiques*, III, 316–17).

54. AN D XXXIX, Dossier 73. Lettre No. 19 (10 mars 1790).

55. AN D XXXIX, Dossier 73. Lettre No. 11 (14 mars 1790).

56. Léger-Limoges, curé of Rouchard, was condemned to death on 12 floréal an I (August 1, 1794). Bussière, *Etudes historiques*, III, 310–11.

57. The sin was taxed at 12 *livres*. Bussière, *Etudes historiques*, III, 310–15.

58. The vicar voluntarily surrendered to the authorities and denied the validity of the charges. The case against him was eventually dismissed. ADD B 1604: Requis du procureur du roi (4 septembre 1790); Information (6 septembre 1790); and Interrogatoire de Pierre Thoury, prêtre et vicaire (10 janvier 1791).

59. Such was the case at Le Bugue, where men armed with knives threatened to open the stomach of the first man to touch the maypole. In Quercy, a similar order given in November, 1791, provoked an insurrection of more than 5,000 peasants who invaded Gourdon on December 3; the next day, a smaller group attacked, pillaged and burned the château du Repaire in the parish of Saint-Aubin-de-Nabirat. Escande, *Histoire de Sarlat*, 284. Also see Bussière, *Etudes historiques*, III, 299–315.

60. Yves-Marie Bercé, *Histoire des Croquants: Etude des soulèvements populaires au XVIIe siècle dans le Sud-Ouest de la France* (Geneva, 1974), 317–23. Also see Bercé, *Croquants et Nu-Pieds* (Paris, 1974).

61. Bercé, *Histoire des Croquants*, 328.

62. Ibid., 403–62.

63. For an elaboration of these themes, see Steven G. Reinhardt, *Justice in the Sarladais, 1770–1790* (Baton Rouge, 1991).

64. Bercé, *Histoire des Croquants*, 632–33. The charivari was a serenade of "rough music" made with kettles, pans, horns, etc., in derision of incongruous marriages. They were usually staged by young men of a parish to express their disapproval, especially of second marriages in which there was a gross disparity in age between the bride and groom. The offending husband was supposed to acknowledge his indiscretion and pay his "fine": treating the participants to food and drink. See Natalie Zemon Davis, *Society and Culture in Early Modern France* (Stanford, 1975), 97–123 ("The Reasons of Misrule").

65. Boutier, "Jacqueries en Pays Croquant," 771.

66. Ibid., 769–71. On the wider issue of why peasant rebellions were less frequent

in the eighteenth century, see Jones, *The Peasantry in the French Revolution*, 40–41, and Emmanuel le Roy Ladurie, "Révoltes et contestations rurales en France de 1675 à 1788," *Annales: Economies, Sociétés, Civilisations* 29 (1974): 6–22.

67. For an elaboration of the potentially subversive use of ritualized inversion, see Davis, *Society and Culture*, 124–51 ("Women on Top"). Also see Sutherland, *France 1789–1815*, 101–03.

68. Boutier, "Jacqueries en pays croquant," 761–62, 780–81; Mona Ozouf, *Festivals and the French Revolution*, trans. Alan Sheridan (Cambridge, Mass., 1988), 232–43.

69. Ozouf, *Festivals and the French Revolution*, 239–40, 243.

70. The former type, "mais individuels" planted to honor or chastise the behavior of certain individuals, was also common in the Périgord. Georges Rocal, *Le Vieux Périgord* (Périgueux, 1926), 205.

71. Such collective maypoles were erected in Burgundy, Picardy, Orléanais, Guyenne, Languedoc, and Franche-Comté. The annual delivery of a maypole was often included in contracts made between villages and large proprietors. As early as 1257, a municipal charter stipulated that the inhabitants of a commune had the right to "quérir le mai" in the woods of the seigneur. Bussière, *Etudes historiques*, III, 259. Nicole Belmont, *Mythes et croyances dans l'ancienne France* (Paris, 1973), 93–95.

72. Bussière, *Etudes historiques*, III, 260, 316–17.

73. Boutier, "Jacqueries en pays croquant," 763–64.

74. Belmont, *Mythes et croyances*, 168–69.

75. Antiseigneurialism contained an implicit challenge to rights of private property in its challenge to agrarian individualism. Jones, *The Peasantry in the French Revolution*, 80–81.

76. Boutier, "Jacqueries en pays croquant," 764–65. During the *quêtes* of the night of Holy Thursday, for example, *la jeunesse* (young people) went singing from door to door, requesting at each lard and chestnuts but especially eggs. If refused, they were known to scale walls and break doors and windows. Georges Rocal, *Vieilles coutumes dévotieuses et magiques du Périgord* (Périgueux, 1971), 126–27; Belmont, *Mythes et croyances*, 83–84.

77. Boutier, "Jacqueries en pays croquant," 772–73.

78. Mikhail Bakhtin, *Rabelais and His World* (Cambridge, Mass., 1968), 10.

79. Belmont, *Mythes et croyances*, 75–76.

80. Ozouf, *Festivals and the French Revolution*, 235.

81. Boutier, "Jacqueries en pays croquant," 772–73; Cameron, *Crime and Repression*, 252–55.

82. For a summary of the disturbances of this era, see Bercé, *Croquants et Nu-Pieds*, 135–39. Also consult Cameron, *Crime and Repression*, 240–41.

83. Most notable was the revival of sectarian violence between Catholics and Huguenots in the region between Nîmes and Montauban. Tackett, *Religion, Revolution, and Regional Culture*, 209; James N. Hood, "Protestant-Catholic Relations and the Roots of the First Popular Counterrevolutionary Movement in France," *Journal of Modern History* 43 (1971): 245–75. For a summary of the events of 1790–91, see Sutherland, *France, 1789–1815*, 108–14.

84. Whereas most provinces with long traditions of peasant unrest supported refractory clergy in 1791, the Périgord and Agenais remained strongly constitutional. Tackett, *Religion, Revolution, and Regional Culture*, 188, 200.

85. Jones, *The Peasantry in the French Revolution*, 40, 119–22.

CLARKE GARRETT

Religion and Revolution in the Midi-Toulousain, 1789–90

HISTORIANS have been slow to acknowledge that the French Revolution differed significantly from region to region, especially in the early years. Admittedly, even during the Old Regime, the region known today as the Midi-Toulousain does not evoke the sense of place of Burgundy or Brittany or Provence. It is a term that was unknown in the eighteenth century, when the departments that comprise it were variously known as Rouergue, Quercy, Upper Languedoc, and the County of Foix. Today it forms the core of the region called Midi-Pyrenees, the administrative center of which is at Toulouse, the region's dominant city since the time of the Gallo-Romans.

During the last several decades, as French governments have begun to move away from their tradition of centralization and to encourage the regional diversity that people in the south had never forgotten, the University of Toulouse has initiated an institute of regional studies, and a substantial portion of the scholarship of its students and faculty has been devoted specifically to the Midi-Toulousain. In the large body of work that French historians (notably Jacques Godechot and his students) have devoted to the region in the French Revolution, they have rejected the possibility that the region — as an entity with distinctive geographical features, economic and social structures, and cultural and political traditions — would therefore have responded to the cataclysm of the French Revolution in ways derived from its specifically regional character. Instead, Godechot contended that a regional emphasis was "incompatible with the French Revolution." Developments might emerge more slowly in the Midi-Toulousain, with a different "rhythm," but they were virtually identical to those in Paris. If instead we follow the lead of Richard Cobb, who has urged that we look at the diversity of responses that local and regional differences

engendered in the crisis that began in 1789, then, perhaps, we shall
see the French Revolution quite differently.[1]

The Midi-Toulousain is just about as varied geographically as the
state of Texas. Extending southward from the lower slopes of the Massif
Central across barren limestone plateaus indented by deep valleys and
gorges, notably those of the Tarn and Lot rivers, then across the great
plain surrounding the cities of Montauban, Albi, and Toulouse, it ends
in a somber patchwork of plateaus, isolated valleys, and foothills that
rise toward the Pyrenees Mountains and the Spanish border.

Travelers, once they have descended from the forests and hills to
the north, have always been struck by the contrast in the appearance
of the countryside, the buildings, and the people of the Midi-Toulousain.
When the English agronomist Arthur Young arrived at Montauban
in 1787, he remarked on the view to the south of "that noble vale, or
rather plain, one of the richest in Europe, which extends on one side
to the sea, and in front to the Pyrenees." Those who have visited Montauban in the age of the automobile will be astonished to learn that
Young saw the white peaks of the Pyrenees themselves, gleaming in
the distance. A seventeenth-century English traveler wrote that while
the northern part of the region was "mountainous and not very fruit-
ful," the rest was "as rich and pleasant as the best provinces in *France.*"

The people of the region, he continued, were "neerer to the tem-
per of the *Spaniards,*" since they were "very devout, great vaunters of
themselves, affecting bravery above their conditions and estates," sav-
ing their money for elegant clothing "so that they may flaunt it in the
street, and be fine on *holydays.*"[2] In 1790, when for a time conflicts
and confrontations in southwestern France made the Midi-Toulousain
the focus of national attention, radical politicians and journalists in
Paris viewed its people similarly: aggressively religious, subject to emo-
tional excess and showy gestures. It must be the climate.[3]

The region was and is as diverse economically as geographically.
In the eighteenth century, the highlands and valleys of Rouergue and
Quercy in the north were inhabited mainly by peasants operating close
to the subsistence level. As in many other poor sections of southern
Europe, there was a scattering of noble proprietors and petty officials,
not much better off economically than the peasants, who therefore
exaggerated every symbol of their social superiority in the small towns

and dispersed *bourgs* of the uplands. The area was also afflicted with a preposterously fragmented judicial system. Rouergue had six hundred separate seigneurial courts, each with its own staff; Cahors, a town of fewer than ten thousand people, had sixty-four different judicial bodies.

The peasants in the highlands between the Toulouse plain and the Pyrenees were no better off, but at least they did not usually have to contend with the exactions of ruthless landlords or quite as large an army of petty officials.[4] On the plains around Montauban and Toulouse, the peasants generally worked as laborers or sharecroppers for rich noble and bourgeois proprietors. Virtually the entire wheat crop was exported; the good quality of the land and aggressive exploitation of it in the eighteenth century enriched the landowners, if not the peasants. Many of the landlords spent most of the year in town, serving as officials of the myriad of administrative and judicial institutions that were central to the economies of both Toulouse and Montauban.[5]

The towns were as varied as the countryside. Toulouse was by far the largest; with fifty-two thousand people it was the eighth largest city in France. Montauban, thirty miles north of Toulouse, was the region's second city, with exactly half Toulouse's population. Castres, primarily a textile town, was third with fourteen thousand. No other town had more than ten thousand people; they included small textile manufacturing centers like Millau and Saint-Affrique and stagnant little places like Pamiers, Cahors, and Rodez, where people remembered with some bitterness their more glorious pasts.

Toulouse was "la sainte, la sage, la sale"— holy, learned, and dirty. The city had had a reputation for piety since the crushing of the Albigensian heresy in the thirteenth century. There were ninety churches and forty-three convents in 1789, and the city's annual cycle of processions on holy days and festival occasions, in which the clergy, royal and municipal officials, and the guilds all participated, was visual evidence of the baroque piety of the Midi. The university had seen better days, but it still provided training in Roman law for the judges and lawyers of the *parlement* of Toulouse, second only to that of Paris in power and reputation, and those in the enormous number of administrative and judicial institutions with which the monarchy had endowed the Midi-Toulousain. Toulouse itself had very little industry, but its parlement, its archbishopric, and the other royal and ecclesiastical bodies gave employment not only to lawyers, clerks, and bureaucrats but also to the servants, artisans, and tradesmen who provided for them.

Montauban was also an important administrative center, with an intendancy, a *Cour des Aides* (royal tax court) and numerous ecclesiastical institutions. Montauban was the most important industrial center in the region with its flour mills, tanneries, and more than sixty manufacturers of rough cloth produced from wool grown and prepared in the hilly uplands in the north, east, and south of the Midi-Toulousain.

Like most of Europe, the region had experienced a substantial population increase in the eighteenth century. Prosperous towns like Toulouse, Montauban, and Castres attracted a continuous flow of immigrants from the poorer rural areas of the Midi-Toulousain. Thus both the economy and migration patterns tended to serve as a framework of cohesion for the diverse region, since its rural hinterlands provided both the raw materials and the working force for the cities.

A transportation system that was highly developed by eighteenth-century standards also served to tie the Midi-Toulousain together. Much of the wheat grown on the plain was exported, either by river to Bordeaux and thence to the American colonies, or by the Canal du Midi from Toulouse to the Mediterranean at Sète. After 1750, the crown, the estates of Languedoc and of Upper Guyenne and several bishops' councils had expended substantial sums on road building. The highway from Cahors to Toulouse was improved; so was the one that connected Montauban with the administrative capital of Lower Languedoc, Montpellier. A network of secondary roads linked all but the most rugged parts of the Rouergue and Foix to the rest of the region.[6]

A final factor both united and divided the Midi-Toulousain. That factor was religion. The region was roughly in the middle of the great crescent across southern France in which Protestants had managed to persist despite 150 years of persecution. Protestants were more numerous to the east of the Midi-Toulousain, in the Cévennes mountains and Lower Languedoc; they were also more numerous to the west, in the Agenais, Poitou, and Périgord. In the Midi-Toulousain, however, they were concentrated in and around a few towns, notably Montauban, Castres, and Millau. In none of them did Protestants comprise more than a fifth or a sixth of the population, but their control of much of the region's textile industry gave both economic influence within the region and important contacts outside it to urban Protestants who had not forgotten that their ancestors had once ruled much of the Midi-Toulousain. There were also Protestants in clusters of villages and small towns of the Rouergue and Foix, linked by commerce and religion to the urban centers. Toulouse and its countryside were almost entirely Catholic, and militantly so. The same could be said of provincial administrative centers like Rodez, Cahors, Albi, and Pamiers. When peasants migrated into the cities of the region, as many did in the eighteenth century, they gravitated toward their coreligionists. Catholics found employment and assistance from Catholic officials and prelates, while Protestant peasants similarly came under the benevolent wing of Protestant consistories and manufacturers.[7]

The enormous flurry of scholarly interest that has accompanied the bicentennial of the French Revolution has produced a growing consensus that the concept of "political culture" helps to explain the origins and development of the Revolution, especially when it is informed — as D. M. G. Sutherland has recently urged — by an analysis of the varied possibilities that regional and local factors provided for the political culture (or political cultures) that emerged. The French Revolution was primarily political, exactly as the revolutionaries themselves believed. Overnight, the events of 1789 transformed political thinking and political rhetoric, while at the same time absorbing into the new politics the social and cultural diversity of Old Regime France.

In the Midi-Toulousain, a combination of national policies, local power struggles, and sectarian dissonance gave traditional religious identities a new importance. Religion tinted every strand of a regional culture that was to become a political culture of a new kind. Religion was not subsumed by the new revolutionary political culture, nor did it become merely the reflection of other, more tangible, social and economic realities. As Harvey Mitchell has warned, one must recognize that the "religious fact" was an autonomous element in the French Revolution, a factor whose "otherness" from the mundane world gives it its significance.[8]

During the sixteenth-century Wars of Religion, Protestants had on several occasions seemed to be on the verge of conquering the entire southwest. Even after it was clear that they would not predominate, they had been willing to use violence to extend their authority beyond their strongholds of Millau, Castres, and Montauban, especially in the terrible second War of Religion of 1621–29. In the ensuing decades, Catholic missionary efforts and royal policies achieved a religious reconquest of the region that climaxed with the revocation of the Edict of Nantes in 1685, but the Protestant minority, although diminished in numbers, excluded from power, and forced to abjure their faith, retained their militancy in the southwest. As in Northern Ireland or Lebanon today, religious identity in the Midi-Toulousain was colored by a tradition of religious violence that continued to punctuate Protestant-Catholic relations. It was along the axis of religiously mixed communities that stretched from Nîmes to Montauban that all the most notorious trials of Protestants that aroused the indignation of the *philosophes* took place. It was there, Timothy Tackett has written, that "the collective memory of past atrocities, the peasant suspicions of the non-conformists and 'outsiders,' and the fundamental fears for the danger to one's soul remained particularly pronounced."[9]

Incidents of actual confrontation were comparatively few in the eighteenth century, but they sufficed to keep the sense of distrust and grievance intense on both sides. Each May 17, the citizens of Toulouse celebrated the expulsion of the Protestants from their city in 1562 with a great procession. In 1762, two months before the bicentennial celebration of the event, Jean Calas, who had been convicted by the parlement of murdering his son for converting to Catholicism, was executed on the Place Saint Georges. The previous year, three Protestant missionaries had been captured north of Montauban near the small town of Caussade, in an area that was roughly half Catholic and half Protestant. While they were being brought under armed guard to Toulouse to be executed, rumors spread through the city that the Protestant peasants of the region were preparing to free the captives by force. The incident served to reawaken the old stereotype of the Protestants as rebels and probable traitors who would if given the opportunity betray France to her Protestant enemies, two of whom (England and Prussia) had just defeated France in the Seven Years' War.[10]

After 1770, the royal authorities tended tacitly to accept the civic existence of Protestants and to ignore their persistence in holding religious assemblies, but the crown made sure that the position of Catholicism as the religion of the state and Catholics' political control of the municipal governments and provincial estates of the southwest were not challenged. As subsequent events would demonstrate, the comparative absence of sectarian violence in the decades before the Revolution was deceptive, since it depended on the crown's ability to maintain the Catholics' predominance, despite the Protestants' increasing economic power and self-confidence.

In 1787, the monarchy responded to the mood of the times and the Protestants' own urging and granted them limited religious toleration. Toleration, however, did not imply equality. The government declared that it would continue to try through "instruction and persuasion . . . to tie together all our subjects by the common profession of the ancient faith of our kingdom." Moreover, Roman Catholicism "will alone enjoy in our realm the rights and honors of public worship." At its last general assembly the following year, the General Assembly of the French Clergy gave cautious approval to the Edict of Toleration, but the assembly professed the hope that "non-Catholics" would continue to be "excluded from the exercise of the rights of patronage and the possession of offices and employments connected with the public order."[11]

In the Midi-Toulousain, where the persistence of a rival faith was a palpable reality, even very limited toleration was distrusted by many in the clergy. Reflecting, they said, the views of their parishioners, they opposed any concessions to the heretics. In the *cahier* of grievances that the clergy of Quercy prepared in 1789 for its deputies to the Estates General to present to the king, they denounced the idea of permitting any public worship other than Roman Catholic and urged him to reconsider his edict of toleration. At Montauban, when a visiting Lenten preacher in a sermon said that all men were created equal, the vicar general berated him, saying that such a notion "smelled of Protestantism." On the other hand, several of the Third Estate's *cahiers* from the Midi-Toulousain called for major ecclesiastical reforms, including severe restrictions on the monastic orders, the turning over of some church property to "the nation's treasury," and (in the *cahier* of Montauban's third estate) a demand that the clergy not involve themselves in "temporal affairs."[12] None of the *cahiers*, it should be noted, advocated political emancipation for the Protestants, as had been proposed at Nîmes and Montpellier in Lower Languedoc.

While the majority of Protestants in the Midi-Toulousain were peasants, it was the urban communities, dominated by wealthy merchants and manufacturers, who had led in pressing for further concessions on the eve of the Revolution. A new generation of Protestant pastors wanted nothing less than full toleration, and the Revolution would make clear that for spokesmen like Jeanbon Saint-André of Montauban and Rabaut Saint-Etienne of Nîmes, religious toleration could be secure only if the Roman Catholics' monopoly of power was broken. Like many of their parishioners, Jeanbon and Rabaut had moved well beyond Calvinist orthodoxy to espouse an advanced form of Voltairean Deism. They had not lost their scorn for the beliefs of their Catholic neighbors, whom Jeanbon in his letters routinely portrayed as "miserable sectarians" duped by fanatical priests.[13]

Even in the Midi-Toulousain, the events of the spring of 1789 produced a mood of euphoria in which old hatreds and rivalries were temporarily forgotten. No Protestants were elected as deputies to the Estates General, but they had participated in the drafting of the *cahiers* and in the municipal revolutions that in July and August overturned local government in many towns and villages. Montauban's leading Protestants, led by Jeanbon Saint-André, worked with "patriot" Catholics to establish a municipal government that supplanted the old one that the bishop had dominated. Toulouse was one of the few major cities that had no kind of municipal revolution, but the *capitouls* (municipal officers) gave their cautious support to the developments of that turbulent summer. In Millau, Louis de Bonald, the future theorist of Catholic absolutism and mayor of the city since 1785, presided over a commission of nobles, clergy, and commoners that not only gave its support to the initiatives of the Constituent Assembly in Paris but also sought to create a confederation with two other leading towns of the Rouergue, Rodez and Villefranche. In villages where the Protestants were in the majority, such as Nègrepelisse near Montauban and Mas d'Azil near Pamiers, they took control of the commune peacefully, with the cooperation of the Catholic minority.[14] Throughout the region Protestants joined, and sometimes dominated, the militias that were formed to cope with the disorders engendered by the collapse of royal authority. It is ironic, considering what was to transpire a few months later, that in the fall of 1789 a newspaper contrasted the "tranquility" of the southwest with the "license" and "brigandage" in other provinces.[15]

In a series of valuable studies of the Revolution in Nîmes, James Hood has shown how a combination of economic crisis, frictions between rival Protestant and Catholic elites, and a municipal power struggle no longer mediated by the crown's authority all served to revive the tradition of sectarian hostility in the community and to polarize religious and political opinion.[16] The same combination of circumstances contributed to heightened tensions in many localities in the Midi-Toulousain. In the first months of 1790, these factors combined with concern over the National Assembly's sweeping reforms of the Roman Catholic church to produce widespread unrest that in May exploded into savage violence between Catholics and Protestants in the streets of Montauban.

The Revolution had abolished the rules by which the game of local politics was played. Power was at issue, but so was religious identity. What Peter Jones has written of the Rouergue holds for much of the Midi-Toulousain: towns and villages were also spiritual communities, "which transcended individual social categories and yet integrated them all."[17] In its reconstruction of political society at national, regional, and local levels, the National Assembly compelled these spiritual communities to define themselves politically. In the Midi-Toulousain, it was the Catholics who took the initiative, calling upon the monarch to preserve the church's special status within France. In many towns and villages, the faction calling themselves "patriots," with whom virtually all of the Protestants were aligned, responded that "counterrevolutionaries" were using "the veil of religion" to disguise what was really "a redoubtable conspiracy by the demons of the aristocracy."[18] The words are those of the first political club in Toulouse, formed in May, 1790, by artisans, merchants, and virtually the entire Protestant community. It would soon play a dominant role in the city's political life.

In fact, in the series of confrontations and riots that rocked southwestern France in 1790 and 1791, the triggers for the violence were specifically religious, responses not only to the actions of the National Assembly that culminated in the Civil Constitution of the Clergy but also to the liturgical rhythms of the Roman Catholic church year. Certainly the episodes had political implications, but to see in them evidence of a counterrevolutionary conspiracy, as "patriots" in both Paris and the southwest tended to do, is to miss part of their significance. Norman Hampson has suggested that to look for a counterrevolution in the confused and contradictory events of the early revolution is an indication "more of good intentions than of good sense." Too many historians, he argues, have unquestioningly accepted the revolutionaries' own conception of a world "where there exist only the Good and the Wicked." Belief in the existence of a counterrevolution was a factor in the Revolution's development from the beginning; it was to be the justification for political conduct on the part of many "patriots" that was tragically at odds with their own principles.[19]

In the capital, a rift within the Revolutionary coalition had begun to appear as early as August, 1789. Religious toleration was one of the divisive issues. A proposal that it be incorporated as a general principle in the Declaration of the Rights of Man and the Citizen had been met by a counterproposal that Catholicism be declared France's state religion. The counterproposal was tabled without discussion. By the time that the National Assembly and the royal family had removed to Paris in October, factions had formed within the assembly, called by their opponents "radicals" or "mad dogs" and "aristocrats" respectively. The latter were in reality a loose coalition whose more prominent members were the group popularly known as the Monarchiens, leading supporters of the National Assembly's first initiatives in the spring who now urged that the Revolution be halted. The king's executive authority should be restored, they declared in a statement of principles, and he should be given control of the royal army and the National Guard. They reaffirmed the principle of religious toleration, but they reminded the public that "the experience of the centuries" taught that civic order and "the interest of the State" required that "the Catholic religion continue to enjoy alone, in the kingdom, the title of National Religion," the only one authorized for public worship.[20]

Jacques-Antoine Cazalès had been elected to the Estates General by the nobility of Rivière-Verdun, between Toulouse and Montauban. In June, he had unwillingly obeyed the king's command and joined the National Assembly. He turned down an invitation to join the Monarchiens, but his position was close to theirs, and it probably reflected as well the views of most of the Catholic elite of landowners and officeholders in the Midi-Toulousain. As religious and other issues polarized the assembly in late 1789, Cazalès emerged as the ablest speaker among those who sat on the right in the National Assembly, but despite the rhetoric of the radical press and orators of the left like Charles and Alexandre Lameth, it is difficult to sustain the view that Cazalès and those who agreed with him supported a "counterrevolution." The term had begun to cover not only the stories of plots against the Revolution and the efforts of the king's brother, the comte d'Artois, to persuade foreign powers to intervene militarily in France, but also the very diverse manifestations of discontent with the course of the Revolution that were being heard in Paris and the provinces.[21]

In October, the comte de Montlosier, a political ally of Cazalès and the Monarachiens, complained that "a thousand false or exaggerated rumors" circulated in Paris. Yet by January even the radical newspaper *Révolutions de Paris* agreed that a counterrevolution seemed impossible, at least if voters repudiated nobles, including former judges and magistrates, and chose true representatives of the people. Both left and right recognized that the municipal elections that were to take place throughout France in February represented a political innovation that could have profound consequences. So did outside observers. William Short, the American government's representative in Paris, observed that "this idea of governing a Kingdom of twenty four millions of inhabitants by municipalities is so new that all opinions respecting it can only be conjectures."[22]

Meanwhile, religious issues continued to arouse controversy in southwestern France. On Christmas Eve, the assembly voted to extend to Protestants full civic rights and access to all public offices and professions. The decree could have profound consequences in the municipalities of the Midi-Toulousain, where the Protestant minority that had once controlled much of the region had been entirely excluded from power for over a century.

In the religiously mixed towns of the region, the considerable expansion of the powers of local government that the National Assembly had decreed, in part in order to dilute the crown's authority, meant that the municipal elections had the potential to alter power relationships between the religious communities. In most towns, however, the moderate coalitions of Catholics and Protestants that had come to prominence in 1789 remained in power, and the religious issue did not yet become politically divisive. The principal exception was Montauban, where (as also happened at Uzès and Nîmes in Lower Languedoc) bitter political rivalries emerged between factions that at least in part defined themselves religiously. As a result, religious antagonism between Protestants and Catholics that had been intense since the sixteenth century became the explosive ingredient when combined with the rivalry between political elites in cities beset by economic distress and the impending disappearance of the royal and ecclesiastical institutions of the Old Regime that had provided employment and status for so many.

Montauban's economic difficulties were severe in early 1790. An extremely cold winter had halted shipping on the Tarn River, throwing the sailors and others involved in shipping out of work, and the nationwide slump in the wool industry meant that many textile workers were unemployed as well. Most disquieting of all, the national administrative reorganization meant that Montauban had lost its intendancy, Cour des Aides, and bishopric, and that henceforth it would be subordinate in the new department of the Lot to its ancient rival, the somber mountain town of Cahors.

One can imagine how all these events must have been seen by the Catholics of Montauban. The political structure had been overturned by those who called themselves patriots, whose leaders included most of the city's textile manufacturers. The disappearance of royal and ecclesiastical institutions meant that a sizeable portion of Montauban's economic base had disappeared. It was out of this volatile mix of traditional religious tension and economic and social crisis that a new political culture was to emerge.

After a bitter contest, the municipal election was won by a slate consisting almost entirely of Catholic landowners and officeholders. No members of the "patriot" committee of 1789 were elected. The Protestants' sole remaining power base was the militia, now integrated into the National Guard. This, too, was challenged, after a wave of château burnings spread across Périgord, Quercy, and the Rouergue in January. New companies of volunteers, consisting entirely of Catholics, had gone out from Montauban to bring the peasants under control. They now sought incorporation into the National Guard. The guard's leaders refused.[23]

There was considerable discontent in Toulouse over the National Assembly's actions, but Protestants were simply too few in number to be seen as a political force, however much they might be disliked by the populace. Unlike Montauban, Toulouse would remain an administrative center, although the parlement, the city's proudest ornament, was to be abolished. Many of the court's officials and staff had long been vocal in their opposition to much that was being enacted in Paris. Nevertheless, however much they and those who depended on them for employment might deplore the direction the Revolution had taken, they were not inclined by temperament or experience to plot violent resistance, nor were they able to propose any genuine alternative in the changed world of 1790. Thus in Toulouse the electors chose a slate of lawyers and merchants, including one Protestant, who supported the new order.[24]

The electoral results were similar in smaller cities in the Midi-Toulousain that were to retain their roles in the new administrative structure and where Protestants were too few to be a factor in the new politics. Thus the electors of Albi, Cahors, and Rodez all chose slates of moderate supporters of the Revolution. Pamiers was the apparent exception; there two factions fought bitterly for control of the fading episcopal town. The faction its rivals called counterrevolutionaries won, but the authorities of the new department of the Ariège reported that there was in fact no counterrevolution at Pamiers. "Private animosities," they wrote, "nourished from generation to generation over the century, have been the sole cause of the troubles that have afflicted this town."[25]

For the Catholics in the Midi-Toulousain, there was however a further cause for discontent when in February the National Assembly abolished monastic vows. The bitterness of the debates led the bishop of Nancy to propose that the assembly assure the nation that it was not hostile to the church as an institution by declaring Roman Catholicism the national religion. Once again, the motion was tabled without discussion. The proposed dissolution of the monasteries may have been especially significant in Languedoc, where reestablishment of convents in Protestant bastions after 1630 had been the first step in the Catholic "reconquest" of the region. Monks and nuns had declined considerably in numbers and influence by 1790, but they continued to have symbolic importance for Protestants and Catholics alike.

In April, Catholic distress came to a head when it was learned that once again the National Assembly had rejected a motion to affirm the special place of the Roman Catholic church in France. This time the proposer was not a deputy on the right but rather Dom Christophe-Antoine Gerle, a Carthusian abbot from the Auvergne, who voted with the left and belonged to the Jacobin club. After the assembly had adjourned for the night, the right gathered its forces at an abandoned

Capuchin monastery to plan a strategy for the next day. Meanwhile, at the Jacobins' meeting that evening, Gerle agreed to withdraw his motion and in its place support a bland substitute. The next morning, after he had done so, several clergy attempted to reintroduce the motion. After a full day of debate, the motion worked out by the Jacobins was passed. Almost immediately, printed copies of Gerle's motion and the minority's declaration of support for it began to circulate throughout France.

It is clear that both sides intended to use the debates over the Gerle motion to arouse popular sentiment. The ensuing six weeks saw a rapid growth in the number of political clubs affiliated with the Paris Jacobins, and opposition to the right's campaign in defense of the special role of the Roman Catholic church in France became the first national issue on which the Jacobin network acted in unison. In the National Assembly the Jacobins' leading orator, Charles Lameth, declared that the campaign on behalf of Catholicism was in fact "the pretext and the signal for the counterrevolutionary insurrection." The "aristocrats," he continued, were distributing copies of their protest throughout France but were concentrating on the south, where religious opinions were "already exalted by the influence of the climate" and the presence of the two "rival religions." The counterrevolutionaries had therefore chosen the Midi as "the most favorable theater" for carrying out their plan, which contemplated nothing less than civil war. The American representative in Paris, William Short, was much more cautious, but he did report to his government that some of those on the right hoped to provoke a schism in the assembly that would compel the king to intervene.[26]

In at least thirty-two communities, ten of them in the Midi-Toulousain, Catholics held assemblies to support the minority statement calling for the affirmation of the special role of their church. Despite the allegations made at the time, it is not likely that the protests were orchestrated either by rightist deputies in Paris or agents of the comte d'Artois. What the protests from the Midi-Toulousain do reveal is a conviction that only Roman Catholicism could hold French society together against the subversive influence of Protestants and *philosophes*. The Catholics of Castres declared that without the cement of religion, society would be "nothing but a shapeless chaos of incoherent and ill-assorted pieces, without connection with each other, and with no relation to the whole." One village in the Rouergue complained that the National Assembly had allowed Protestants to "insult the Catholics at will and to attempt to dominate them. Was it any wonder that the people were now beginning to lose confidence in all the Revolution's decrees?"[27]

In Montauban, where the political situation continued to be exacerbated by the continuing stalemate between the municipality and the National Guard over the status of the volunteer companies that the Protestants scornfully called the "Romanist" legions, there were several meetings that produced a printed declaration by the "assembled Catholics of Montauban" and an extensive correspondence with other towns in the southwest. In communities along the "Nîmes-Montauban axis" of Protestant-Catholic tensions, the reorganization of the Roman Catholic church, the "attack" on the monasteries, the granting of civic equality to Protestants, and the impending sale of church property presaged nothing less than the destruction of their religion, for which (the Catholics of Montauban declared) they were willing to "shed their last drop of blood."[28]

There were also several assemblies of Catholics in Toulouse. They received no support from the municipal government, which deplored the existence "in the bosom of Toulouse" of a party "hostile to the regeneration of France." The authorities of the department of the Haute-Garonne concurred. They were afraid that in Toulouse, always "too disposed to fanaticism," the combination of religious and economic discontent would lead to an intensification of the violence that had already led to several deaths on the streets of the city in clashes between unemployed workers and dependants of the old parlement. When an armed crowd pursued some "patriots" after one Catholic assembly, the municipality prohibited any further meetings.[29]

Despite the municipality's action, the radical press worried that Toulouse, the city "which saw the virtuous Calas perish on the scaffold," was still being inundated with "pamphlets, incendiary sermons, indulgences, and retreats." The *Courrier de Paris* printed several subversive prayers that were being circulated, including an "*Amende honorable* at the foot of the cross" that concluded "Sweet Jesus! . . . France has become a vast Calvary." To the radical press, religion was merely the pretext for "saintly masquerades"—like the penitential processions of religious confraternities and a pilgrimage to a chapel commemorating the crusade against the Albigensian heretics — that the clergy would use in order to arouse the superstitious populace against the Revolution. The newspapers failed to note that it was the Lenten season, which annually featured such activities. In fact, there is evidence that prominent clergy in Toulouse discouraged religious activities among the laity that might have political implications.[30]

Whether because of the actions of the clergy and the governmental authorities or because of the scarcity of actual Protestants, it was not at Toulouse that religious and political hostilities exploded into violence, but at Montauban.[31] The occasion was the Rogation Day procession on May 10, 1790. Throughout the spring, the friction between Protestants and Catholics had been played out against a backdrop of the festivals and ceremonies of the church year. There had been the annual series of Lenten sermons, which surely addressed the present religious crisis; there had been a great procession on Palm Sunday, in which all the corporations and institutions of the Catholic community provided a visual representation of the hierarchies and interactions of church and state that the Revolution was in the process of transforming; then came Easter, the central festival of the liturgical year. There was a rogation procession on Saint Mark's Day, April 25, and then, early on the morning of Monday, May 10, the first of the three processions that preceded Ascension Thursday.

The rogation processions were distinct among the major liturgical processions because they were penitential, calling upon God to spare humankind the wrath it so richly deserved. With a great crucifix at its head, the procession, led by the clergy, followed by the laity, men and women alike, would have gone through the town and into the countryside to pray that this harvest would be good. Traditionally, crosses would have been placed in the fields to symbolize the divine blessing that the rogation liturgy invoked. The procession would then have completed the circuit and returned to town. Everything about the rogation procession — the crucifix, the liturgy with its echoes of pre-Christian agrarian religion, even the fact of procession itself — partook of a mental world to which the Protestant merchants, manufacturers, and artisans of Montauban could never belong.[32]

At the conclusion of the procession, apparently the clergy reminded the crowd that on that very day officers of the municipality were to enter Montauban's convents and monastic houses in order to take an inventory of their possessions as mandated by the National Assembly. It was suggested that groups of women place themselves in front of the gates of the religious houses in order to prevent it. One can assume that all of this had been prepared on the day before, Sunday, by sermons in the churches followed by discussions in cabarets and as people promenaded on the plazas and broad avenues of Montauban. Also on Sunday, the municipal authorities had met for four hours with leaders of the National Guard and the heads of the city's most prominent Protestant families in an unsuccessful attempt to resolve the question of the incorporation of the Catholic companies into the Guard.

At this point, both sides seem to have recognized that ancient religious hostilities and political rivalries were converging in a struggle for control of the municipality. A week earlier, Jeanbon Saint-André had written Poncet-Delpech, Montauban's representative in the National Assembly, that the Catholics claimed that "religion [was] in danger, the heretics ready to seize all places" in the municipal government.[33]

When the municipal officials arrived at the convents at eleven that Monday morning and found the women there, they quickly withdrew. It is difficult to believe that they had not anticipated some such protest when they scheduled their visits for a Catholic religious holiday. A crowd also went to the home of the baron Du Puy-Montbrun, the commander of the National Guard and a Catholic, and threatened to burn down his house unless he "abandoned the party of the Protestants."[34]

It is clear that some sort of protest had been orchestrated, probably with the participation of the clergy and at least some members of the municipal government. No one in the elite, however, anticipated what now transpired. Early in the afternoon, as representatives of the municipality and the National Guard continued to try to resolve their differences, the Catholics met at the Church of the Cordeliers to prepare another address protesting the dissolution of the monasteries. Someone rushed into the church and announced that the Protestants had occupied the Hôtel de Ville (town hall). Convinced that they were preparing to seize the city by force, the crowd rushed to confront them.

What in fact had happened was that about fifty national guardsmen, members of the dragoons or mounted infantry and nearly all of them Protestants, had on their own initiative decided to go to the Hôtel de Ville to prevent the arms stored there from falling into the hands of an angry Catholic crowd. Confronted now with just such a crowd, a few of the dragoons rashly fired upon them. By the time that municipal leaders had arrived and tried to intercede, it was too late. "In an instant and by a sudden eruption," a witness named Jacques Delbreil wrote in his memoirs, "the multitude penetrated into the court-yard of the Hôtel de Ville." The dragoons fled into the building, and for two hours the crowd continued to attack, armed with sticks, stones, and a few muskets and sabres. By the time royal troops arrived from the edge of town, five guardsmen were dead and many others wounded. Several of the corpses had been mutilated, and one had been dragged to the victim's home and left exposed there. It was, Delbreil, wrote, "an accidental collision that could not have been prevented and that it was impossible to prevent."[35]

It was also disturbing evidence that, in the right circumstances, the horrors of religious violence could still erupt two full centuries after the end of the Wars of Religion. The troops and the municipality managed to prevent further bloodshed, but they agreed to allow the crowd to end the terrible day that had begun with a religious procession with another one. The dragoons were compelled to remove their uniform jackets and their hats with the national cockade. They were then paraded through the streets to the plaza in front of the cathedral. It was an *amende honorable*, a ritual of public humiliation, one that their Protestant ancestors had had to perform in the centuries of persecution. The fact that these guardsmen were dragoons, the troops whose depredations had been so effective a century earlier in Louis XIV's campaign to force Protestants in Montauban and elsewhere to convert to Roman Catholicism, was surely not lost on any of those present.

Many of Montauban's Protestants fled to other towns in the Midi-Toulousain where they had family and business connections. Their exodus caused severe dislocation of the already crippled local economy, but nonetheless order was quickly restored. The municipality urged the Protestants to return and called on the clergy to preach "peace, tolerance, and charity." The municipal authorities insisted that they were loyal to the National Assembly, and at the great national cele-

bration on July 14 presided over the patriotic *Te Deum* and the blessing of the flags of a National Guard that now was thoroughly (if temporarily) Catholic.

There was no further violence, save for a minor confrontation on
the Catholic holiday of Pentecost between Catholics and those Protestants who had not fled the town. Instead of the red, white and blue
cockade of the Revolution, the Catholics of Montauban wore a white
cockade surmounted by a cross. The leaders of the "Assembly of Catholics," meanwhile, continued to correspond with their counterparts in
Nîmes and other towns, even proposing at one point a sort of Albigensian crusade in reverse, in which the Catholics of southern France,
"wearing the cross on their clothing as a sure sign of what they carried
in their hearts," would liberate the north from those who were preparing to destroy the Catholic monarchy of France.[36]

Reactions to the events in Montauban varied. Other municipalities in the Midi-Toulousain either spoke out against the conduct of Montauban's authorities or remained noncommittal. The National Guard
of Bordeaux meanwhile launched a crusade of its own, sending a small
army of volunteers to join a troop of national guards who wished to
"liberate" Montauban from its oppressors. The citizens of Montauban
resolved to resist, recalling how their city had successfully held off a
beseiging army led by the king himself in 1629.[37] They had apparently
forgotten that in 1629 Montauban had been entirely Protestant. The
National Assembly responded by dispatching the marquis de Lafayette's
aide-de-camp, Mathieu Dumas, to mediate in order to avert the civil
war that Paris believed was developing in the southwest between Protestants and Catholics, "patriots" and "aristocrats."

Within the Midi-Toulousain itself, nothing of the sort seemed im-
minent. There had been a protest march at Castres, also on May 10,
but it came to nothing. Otherwise the region remained calm. In Lower
Languedoc, especially at Nîmes and Uzès where the relations between
Catholics and Protestants were even worse than at Montauban, there
were continued confrontations that climaxed at Nîmes in June when
after several days of violence Protestant peasants from the Cévennes
mountains north of the city intervened on the side of their coreligionists. In the *bagarre* (affray) that followed, three hundred died, nearly
all of them Catholics. The savagery rivaled that of the Wars of Religion.

At Montauban, Dumas succeeded in securing the release of Protestant prisoners, despite the protests of "furious fanatics" who surrounded the prison. He concluded that the municipality was "embarrassed" by the situation and eager to see its conclusion. He also met with representatives of leading Protestant families and urged them not to encourage the sort of armed intervention that was about to erupt at Nîmes. He went on to Toulouse, where he similarly dissuaded National Guard companies that included Protestants aroused by the incendiary sermons of Jeanbon Saint-André, who had fled to the city from Montauban on May 10. "It is the day of vengeance," Jeanbon told Dumas, "for which we have been waiting above a hundred years."[38]

The National Assembly asked Pierre-Jacques Vieillard, a deputy from Normandy, to present a report on the Montauban crisis and to make recommendations. Based on the eyewitness accounts now deposited in the departmental archives at Montauban, the report is generally excellent. Curiously, it barely mentions religion as having been a factor and does not mention the *amende honorable* with which May 10 had ended, perhaps because its religious resonances were too obviously out of line with the National Assembly's insistence that the Montauban events had been a political conflict between patriots and counterrevolutionaries. Vieillard was careful not to suggest the complicity of the municipality in what had transpired. Nevertheless, because of its failure to control the crisis, he recommended that it be replaced by a new municipal government appointed by the departmental authorities. The National Assembly concurred; they also transferred the Regiment of Languedoc, which had shown itself openly sympathetic to the Catholics, and replaced it with the securely revolutionary Regiment of Touraine. Although the municipality protested that they had been the "saviors" of Montauban from further violence after May 10, they accepted without resistance their replacement by a government that was half Protestant.[39]

Jeanbon Saint-André went from Toulouse to Bordeaux, where his Protestant and commercial connections gave him access to that city's new political leadership. He remained there until the fall of 1790. His letters show that he was convinced that the events of May 10 had been part of a plot and that the municipal government was behind it. For him as for many middle-class Protestants in the Midi-Toulousain, the faith of their Calvinist forbears was something of an embarrassment. They shared the memory of the Protestants' former glory and more recent oppression, but religious zeal was a vestige of more ignorant times, something that survived only among Catholics. Thus, the Protestants contended, the campaign to "save religion" had been only a pretext. Their political rivals had cynically aroused the Catholic masses in order to keep the true patriots from power.[40]

There was sporadic street violence in Montauban throughout the fall of 1790, which the victorious patriot faction interpreted as further evidence that the majority of the city persisted in its commitment to the destruction of the Revolution. They may have been quite sincere in their belief in the existence of a continuing counterrevolutionary threat, but the interrogations of the nearly three hundred suspects rounded up in Montauban during the Reign of Terror suggest instead that there was virtually no organized opposition after August of 1790. The Protestant and patriot minority was in full control, supported by the forces of the restored National Guard and the Regiment of Touraine. They organized a political club that met in elegant quarters in the former palace of the Cour des Aides. The club maintained close contacts with the Jacobin club in Paris and with their counterparts in Toulouse and other towns in the Midi-Toulousain. Many of the wealthier Catholics in Montauban either retired to their country estates or went to Toulouse, which despite the sporadic turbulence of the spring had now become a haven of political calm. The opposition that remained in Montauban responded as losing factions generally did in the Midi. They simply abstained from participation in politics, nursing their grievances in private and awaiting a better opportunity.[41]

The establishment of the Civil Constitution of the Clergy caused sporadic protests throughout the Midi-Toulousain in 1791, frequently coinciding with major occasions in the Catholic liturgical year such as Lent, Epiphany, and Corpus Christi. Virtually nowhere in the Midi-Toulousain did a majority of the Catholic clergy take the oath of allegiance to the new civil constitution of the clergy. In religiously mixed towns like Millau and Saint-Affrique in the department of the Aveyron and Lavaur in the Tarn, the percentage of clergy taking the oath was less than ten percent. Throughout the region, Catholics tended to see the Civil Constitution as further evidence, as if more were needed, that the Protestants intended to destroy their church. Only gradually in the course of 1791 did some of the protests, mainly in the mountainous areas of the Aveyron and the Tarn, begin to merge with the currents of popular counterrevolution that were developing in south-eastern France.[42]

If there was a conspiracy in 1791, it was organized not by the Catholics but by the Protestants. At Montauban, Saint-Affrique, and Millau, three towns in which Protestant merchants had extensive commercial and family connections, the victorious political faction showed it was prepared to tolerate no opposition. They continually complained of the plotting of local "counterrevolutionaries" and "fanatics," but in all three towns a coalition of Protestants and those Catholics whom other Catholics decried as "renegades" would be in full control for the next four years.

In August of 1791, there began a series of incidents in which gangs of youths threatened Catholic opponents of the local regimes or vandalized their property in order to force them to leave town. At Montauban, the first incidents coincided with Jeanbon Saint-André's presidency of the Jacobin club and the political eclipse within the club of manufacturers and merchants by more radical shopkeepers and artisans, also largely Protestants. Among those who complained to the departmental authorities that they had been visited by these so-called "black bands" were a prominent manufacturer who had belonged to the municipal government at the time of the riots of May 10, 1790; the printer who had produced most of the Catholic propaganda disseminated that spring; and a departmental official in the district administration of Montauban. They complained that these incidents were becoming a daily occurrence. They also said that the municipal government and National Guard either looked the other way or in some cases took an active part. When the department admonished the municipality for allowing such incidents to take place, the Montauban Jacobins warned that the city was still in danger of experiencing a return to the chaos of 1790 because the Catholics—those who opposed "*the Diversity of Religious opinions*" and had tried "to drown the Constitution and its Defenders in torrents of blood"—were still unreconciled to the new order.[43]

In 1990, the notion that in a revolutionary situation a political opposition must necessarily constitute a counterrevolution has been abandoned, even in the former People's Republics of Hungary, Czechoslovakia, and Romania. Unfortunately, even today most French historians of the Revolution in the southwest tend to produce a caricature of the regional confrontation of 1790. One historian writes of "a strong, prudent, yet firm Protestant bourgeoisie" that suddenly found itself (at Nîmes) confronted by a Catholic populace "aroused by demagogues and seemingly dredged up from the depths of the sixteenth century." Another says that the Protestants, having defeated their counterrevolutionary opponents and won control of the region, "applied their qualities of order and intelligence" to administering it.[44]

I would suggest instead that the victorious "patriot" faction that included virtually all the Protestants in the region had succeeded in creating a very effective revolutionary political culture. It combined the rhetoric of Enlightenment idealism with a scenario of counterrevolutionary plotting by Catholics and "aristocrats" that justified the seizure of all the levers of power. It used that power against expressions of dissent — some of which, admittedly, were violent — that were primarily religious in content, especially in those areas of the Midi-Toulousain where Protestants and Catholics remembered two hundred years' history of rivalry, confrontation, and violence.

The events in Montauban in the spring of 1790 convinced the Protestants and their allies that the Catholic majority would never accept either the political equality of Protestants or the spiritual eclipse of Catholicism without coercion. The opposition's response, on the other hand, demonstrates that they had failed to fabricate a political culture that could successfully confront the "patriots," either politically or ideologically. Like the deputies of the right in the National Assembly, the Catholic elite could protest; it could seek to preserve something of the past within the revolutionary context; but when the outcome was savage violence, as at Montauban and Nîmes, it may have frightened them as much as it did the victorious radicals.

NOTES

1. Jacques Godechot, *La Révolution française dans le Midi-toulousain* (Toulouse, 1986), 10, 107; Richard Cobb, *The Police and the People: French Popular Protest 1789–1820* (Oxford, 1970), xvi. I have explored these questions more fully in "The Problem of the Midi in French Revolutionary Historiography," *Consortium on Revolutionary Europe: Proceedings 1989* (Athens, Ga., 1990).

2. Arthur Young, *Travels in France and Italy* (1915; reprint London: Everyman's Library, 1976), 27; Peter Heylayn quoted in Charles Tilly, *The Contentious French* (Cambridge, Mass., 1986), 69.

3. Alexandre Lameth, *Histoire de l'Assemblée constituante* (Paris, 1828), I, 198;

see also *Le Courrier de Paris dans les Provinces*, April 14, 1790, p. 130; *Réimpression de l'ancien Moniteur* IV (May 4, 1790), 287; Camille Desmoulins, *Oeuvres* (Munich, 1980), III, 519.

4. Peter Jones, *Politics and Rural Society: The Southern Massif Central (1750–1880)* (Cambridge, 1985), 78–81; Martyn Lyons, "M.-G.-A. Vadier (1736–1828): The Formation of the Jacobin Mentality," *French Historical Studies* 10 (1977): 77.

5. Robert Forster, *The Nobility of Toulouse in the Eighteenth Century: A Social and Economic Study* (Baltimore, 1960), 32–42; Georges Frêche, *Toulouse et la Région Midi-Pyrénées au siècle des lumières (vers 1670–1789)* (Toulouse, 1974), 779; Daniel Ligou, "Montauban des Lumières," *Histoire de Montauban* (Toulouse, 1984), 176; Archives départementales du Tarn-et-Garonne (hereafter cited as ADTG), L97.

6. Frêche, *Toulouse et la Région*, 644–45; Godechot, *Midi-toulousain*, 8–10; Forster, *The Nobility of Toulouse*, 67–69; Jones, *Massif Central*, 25–29; *Histoire de Pamiers* (Pamiers, 1981), 295–96.

7. Alice Wemyss, *Les Protestants du Mas-d'Azil: Histoire d'une résistance 1680–1830* (Toulouse, 1961), 112–13; Jones, *Massif Central*, 67–69.

8. D. M. G. Sutherland, introduction to "Special Issue: The French Revolution," *French Historical Studies* 16 (1989): 259–61; Lynn Hunt, *Politics, Culture and Class in the French Revolution* (Berkeley, 1984), 2–3, 12–15; Harvey Mitchell, preface to Janos M. Bak and Gerhard Benecke, eds., *Religion and Rural Revolt: Papers Presented to the Fourth Interdisciplinary Workshop on Peasant Studies* (Manchester, 1984), 73.

9. Timothy Tackett, *Religion, Revolution, and Regional Culture in Eighteenth-Century France: The Ecclesiastical Oath of 1791* (Princeton, 1986), 209.

10. David Bien, *The Calas Affair: Persecution, Toleration, and Heresy in Eighteenth-Century Toulouse* (Princeton, 1960), 50, 77–88; Robert Schneider, *Public Life in Toulouse, 1463–1789* (Ithaca, 1989), 91; Antoine de Cathala-Couture, *Histoire politique, ecclésiastique et littéraire du Querci* (Montauban, 1788), III, 128–34.

11. Quoted in Burdette C. Poland, *French Protestantism and the French Revolution: A Study in Church and State, Thought and Religion, 1685–1815* (Princeton, 1957), 79–80, 85.

12. Leon Lévy-Schneider, *Le conventionnel Jeanbon Saint-André* (Paris, 1901), 56–57 and n.7; vicar general quoted from a pamphlet in ibid., 49n; *Cahiers de doléances de la sénéchaussée de Montauban et du pays at jugérie de Rivière-Verdun pour les Etats-généraux de 1789* (Montauban, 1925), xi, 17, 18–22, 58, 65, 72.

13. Marcel Reinhard, *Religion, Révolution et Contre-Révolution* (Paris, 1960), 52–54, 145–47; M. A. Lods, ed., "Documents inédits: Correspondance de Jeanbon Saint-André avec Lasource," *Révolution française* 21 (1882): 364; Daniel Ligou, "Jeanbon Saint-André et la journée du 10 mai 1790 à Montauban," *Annales historiques de la Révolution française* 22 (1949–50): 237.

14. Martyn Lyons, *Revolution in Toulouse: An Essay in Provincial Terrorism* (Bern, 1978), 33–34; Ligou, "Montauban des lumières," 33–34; Lévy-Schneider, *Jeanbon*, 57–60; Jean-Marie Carbasse, "Louis de Bonald et la Confédération des villes du Rouergue (8 aout 1789)," in *Histoire du Languedoc: Actes du 110e Congrès national des sociétés savantes, section d'histoire moderne et contemporaine* (Paris: CTHS, 1985), II, 191–95; Wemyss, *Mas d'Azil*, 216–20; Pierre Dordonné, *L'Ivre de politique: Nègrepelisse entre protestants et catholiques* (Montauban, 1982), 22–25.

15. *Le Journal de la généralité de Montpellier*, quoted in Robert Laurent and Geneviève Gavignaud, *La Révolution française dans le Languedoc mediterranéen 1789–1799* (Toulouse, 1987), 56.

62   CLARKE GARRETT

16. James Hood, "Protestant-Catholic Relations and the Roots of the First Popular Counterrevolutionary Movement in France," *Journal of Modern History* 43 (1971): 247–50; "Permanence des conflits traditionnels sous la Révolution: l'exemple du Gard," *Revue d'histoire moderne et contemporaine* 24 (1977): 602–40; "Revival and Mutation of Old Rivalries in Revolutionary France," *Past and Present* 82 (1979): 82–115; "Disorders in a Power Vacuum," *Consortium on Revolutionary Europe: Proceedings 1976* (Athens, Ga., 1978), 16–28.

17. Jones, *Politics and Rural Society*, 94.

18. Archives départementales de l'Haute Garonne (ADHG), Sociéte littéraire et patriotique de Toulouse, May 6 and May 20, 1790, L4542.

19. Norman Hampson, "La contre-révolution a-t-elle existé?" in *Les résistances à la Révolution: Actes du colloque de Rennes (17–21 septembre 1985)*, ed. François Lebrun and Roger Dupuy (Paris, 1987), 462–68.

20. Quoted in Augustin Challamel, *Les Clubs, comités, sociétés, salons, réunions, cafés, restaurants et libraires* (1895; reprint New York, 1974), 104. See also Louis Gottschalk and Margaret Maddox, *Lafayette in the French Revolution: From the October Days through the Federation* (Chicago, 1973), 151; and Timothy Tackett, "Nobles and Third Estate in the Revolutionary Dynamic of the National Assembly, 1789–1790," *American Historical Review* 94 (1989): 285–88.

21. *Historical Dictionary of the French Revolution* (1983), s.v. "Cazalès," by Paul H. Beik, Cf. *Critical Dictionary of the French Revolution* (1989), s.v. "Revolutionary Assemblies," by Denis Richet.

22. Francois Reynaud de Montlosier, *Mémoires* (Paris, 1830), I, 313; *Révolutions de Paris*, January 9–16, 1790; William Short to John Jay, January 23, 1790, in Julian P. Boyd, ed., *The Papers of Thomas Jefferson* (Princeton, 1961), XVI, 121.

23. Peter Jones, *The Peasantry in the French Revolution* (Cambridge, 1988), 70–78; Eugene Sol, *La Révolution en Quercy* (Paris, 1929–32), I, 310–14; ADTG, Fonds Forestié 534, Jacques Delbreil, "Mémoires sur les affaires du 10 mai 1790."

24. Lyons, *Toulouse*, 34; Lenard R. Berlanstein, *The Barristers of Toulouse in the Eighteenth Century (1740–1793)*, (Baltimore, 1975), 160–65.

25. Quoted in Lyons, "Vadier," 83; Henri Enjalbert, "Le choc révolutionnaire (1788–1802)," in *Histoire de Rouergue* (Toulouse, 1979), 276–80; Jean Favry, "L'entrée dans la politique moderne," in *Histoire d'Albi* (Toulouse, 1983), 228–30.

26. Michael L. Kennedy, *The Jacobin Clubs in the French Revolution: The First Years* (Princeton, 1982), 153; Lameth, *Histoire*, II, 198–99; William Short to John Jay, April 23, 1790, *The Papers of Thomas Jefferson* XVI, 371–73.

27. Archives départementales du Tarn, L558; Rouergue village assembly quoted in Tackett, *Religion, Revolution, and Regional Culture*, 217.

28. Archives nationales (hereafter cited as AN), F7 3692, doss. Haupila.

29. Quoted in David Higgs, *Ultraroyalism in Toulouse: From Its Origins to the Revolution of 1830* (Baltimore, 1973), 28.

30. *Révolutions de Paris*, April 24–May 1, 1790; *Courrier de Paris*, April 29 and May 7, 1790; Archives municipales de Toulouse (hereafter cited as AMT), 5S48, abbé de Cambon, vicaire général de Toulouse, to unknown, April 14, 1790.

31. My account of the riots of May 10 is based on the following contemporary accounts: Pierre-Jacques Vieillard, *Rapport fait à l'Assemblée nationale dans la séance de 22 juillet dernier, au nom du comité des rapports, sur les troubles souvenus dans la ville de Montauban* (Paris, 1790); documents printed in Antoine Ombret, Jean-Claude Fau and René Touron, eds., *La Révolution en Bas-Quercy* (Montauban, 1973); Jeanbon

Saint-André's letters, ed. Daniel Ligou, "Jeanbon Saint-André et la journée du 10 mai 1790 à Montauban," *Annales historiques de la Révolution française* 22 (1949–50): 229–40; AN doss. Haupila, F7 3692; and eyewitness accounts collected in ADTG, L199, L222, and 7H37.

32. *New Catholic Encyclopedia* (1967), s.v. "Rogation Days" and "Processions"; *Histoire de la France rural* (Paris, 1975), I, 546–47. On the special significance of Rogation Day processions, see Natalie Z. Davis, "The Sacred and the Body Social in Sixteenth-Century Lyon," *Past and Present* 90 (1981): 57–58.

33. Jeanbon Saint-André to Poncet-Delpech, May 3, 1790, in Odette Ligou, ed., "Documents sur la campagne anti-protestante à Montauban pendant le printemps de 1790," *Congrès régional des fédérations historiques de Languedoc (Carcassonne 24–26 mai 1952)* (Carcassonne, 1952), 179. For a very different account of the causes of the May 10 events, which insists they were part of a counterrevolutionary plot, see Daniel Ligou, "Le monde contre-révolutionnaire à Montauban," in *Religion, Révolution, Contre-Révolution dans le Midi 1789–1799* (Nîmes, 1990), 51–56.

34. ADTG, liasse 9, 7H37 and L199.

35. ADTG, Fonds Forestié 534, Delbreil, "Mémoires."

36. Pierre Arches, "La fête de la fédération en 1790 dans la commune de Montauban," *Actes du 79ᵉ congrès national des sociétés savantes. Alger 1954* (Paris, 1955), 93–102; "Proclamation des messieurs le maire et les officiers municipaux de la ville de Montauban (31 mai 1790)," in Ombret, ed., *Bas-Quercy*, I, 4; AN, doss. Haupila, F7 3692.

37. AMT, *Extrait des registres de la maison commune de la ville de Bordeaux 15 mai 1790* (Bordeaux, 1790); ADTG, Fonds Forestié 534, Delbreil, "Mémoires."

38. Mathieu Dumas, *Memoirs of His Own Time* (London, 1839), I, 174.

39. *Moniteur*, IV, 408, and V, 236–37.

40. Ligou, ed., "Jeanbon Saint-André et la journée du 10 mai," 235, 240; Lévy-Schneider, *Jeanbon*, 73. Cf. Daniel Ligou, who continues to insist on Jeanbon's moderation, most recently in *Jeanbon Saint-André, membre du Grand Comité de Salut Public (1749–1813)* (Paris, 1989), 39–40.

41. ADTG, L99; ADHG, L4542, Société littéraire et patriotique de Toulouse, October 16 and 19, 1790; AMT, 2I31, Registre de retractions ou désaveu des signatures surpris aux citoyens de Toulouse; Georges Fournier, "Traditions municipales et vie politique en 1789," in *Droite et Gauche de 1789 à nos jours* (Montpellier, 1975), 77–80. Cf. Ligou, "Le monde contre-révolutionnaire à Montauban," 56–58.

42. Tackett, *Religion, Revolution, and Regional Culture*, 219, 295, and appendix II; Archives départementales de l'Aveyron, *Répertoire numérique de la série L*, ed. Jean-Marie Tissergue (Rodez, 1977), 17–18; Jones, *Politics and Rural Society*, 196–98; Anarcharsis Combes, *Histoire de la ville de Castres et des ses environs pendant la Révolution française* (Castres, Granier, 1875), 64–66.

43. ADTG, L404, August 21, 1791; Archives départementales du Lot, L231, August 13–October 3, 1791; Lévy-Schneider, *Jeanbon*, 98; Peter Jones, "Political Commitment and Rural Society in the Southern Massif Central," *European Studies Review* 10 (1980): 347–48; Sol, *La Révolution en Quercy*, IV, 26.

44. *Critical Dictionary of the French Revolution*, s.v. "Civil Constitution of the Clergy," by Mona Ozouf; Jean Sentou, "Révolution et contre-révolution," *Histoire du Languedoc* (Toulouse, 1967), 465.

RODERICK PHILLIPS

Remaking the Family: The Reception of Family Law and Policy during the French Revolution

AMONG THE MANY TASKS undertaken by the legislators of the French Revolution, perhaps the most ambitious was the remaking of the French family. This is not to say that enterprises such as giving France a constitution (or three), reforming the legal and fiscal systems, and reorganizing the church and the army were conceptually straightforward or easily executed. But remaking the family, the basic institution of eighteenth-century society, meant confronting a peculiar set of obstacles. The reform of family law was a beginning, and the elaboration of a revolutionary family ideology, was another step, but modifying actual attitudes and behavior within the family meant challenging relationships of the most fundamental kinds: between men and women, between parents and children, between siblings, and between the individual and the family group. To attempt to reform such relationships was to bring the Revolution down to the most fundamental levels of French society.

As daunting as it was, such a revolution in the family was the implicit or explicit goal of many of the policies adopted by successive French regimes between 1789 and 1799. We should recognize at the outset, however, that it is hazardous to generalize about the ideologies and models of the family that were promoted throughout a ten-year period that was marked by rapid and frequent changes of dominant political and social ideology. Although the reform of the family was on the agenda in each phase of the Revolution, the substance of reform tended to mirror the prevailing ideology.

We should begin, then, by outlining the scope of family reform as it was implied by changes in family law, and explicitly articulated in the rhetoric of the Revolution.[1] In the early phase of the Revolution

(1789–91), the changes in family law tended toward the elimination of the arbitrariness of power that was associated with the Old Regime family. Private arrest warrants (*lettres de cachet*) which had been used to imprison children and wives guilty of no crime, but of behaving in a manner offensive to the honor of their families, were abolished. The power of husbands over wives (*puissance maritale*) was trimmed by the imposition of fines and imprisonment specifically for assaulting a woman. The power of fathers over children (*puissance paternelle*) was limited by the gradual reform of inheritance laws that eventually made equal inheritance by all children mandatory. In 1790 a new family court (*tribunal de famille*) was established. It was composed of relatives, friends, or neighbors of the parties to a dispute (any dispute between family members came within its competence), and it brought the exercise of family authority within a formal, if familial, framework, thus reducing paternal authority even further. The general effect of these reforms was to undermine the patriarchal family of the Old Regime, to confine the authority of the father within legal bounds, and to provide a measure of security for wives and children. The parallel between these measures and the transformation of royal power from the Old Regime to the constitutional monarchy is striking: in a metaphorical sense the paterfamilias (husband/father) who had wielded authority akin to that of the king in the Old Regime family found himself limited by the rights of other family members.[2]

In the next phase of the Revolution, family law reform went even further. The Constitution of 1791 declared that marriage was no more than a civil contract, and this principle was embodied in important legislation that was passed on September 20, 1792. This law secularized marriage, legalized divorce, gave women legal equality in marriage, and established the civil records (*état civil*) that would replace the parish registers. Not only did these measures represent an attack on Catholic doctrines of marriage (especially the legalization of divorce), but they removed jurisdiction over the family from the church. The net effect of this law, passed a month after the suspension of the monarchy and two days before the proclamation of the First Republic, was to secularize and extend the principles of liberty and equality to family law. As for fraternity, it was embodied in an ethic of family harmony that was promoted in various ways. The Festivals of Marriage (*Fêtes des Epoux*), for example, extolled the personal and social benefits of marriage and family life, and stressed the virtues of marital fidelity and filial piety.

In the most radical phase of the Revolution, from mid-1793 to mid-1794, changes were made to family law that might be interpreted as an attempt to destroy traditional family relationships. For a short time, illegitimate children were given rights of inheritance equal to those of legitimate children, adoption was legalized, and divorce was facilitated in a way that invited abuse. Such laws did not last, however, and despite qualms often expressed during the Directory (1795–99), the reforms of family law put in place between 1789 and 1792 were maintained until the Napoleonic period. At that time legal reforms reflected a shift to a less egalitarian, more authoritarian, and male-dominated family system.

Despite the variations from phase to phase and the aberrant policies of 1793–94, the thrust of family reform throughout the Revolution was generally coherent. It aimed to create a family that was congruent with the regenerated sociey that the Revolution aimed to confer on France. In no way did it seek to destroy family authority, as some critics have suggested, but it sought to limit authority and make it accountable, just as the revolutionaries had rid France of the arbitrary authority of the Old Regime. As for the family relationships envisaged by the revolutionaries, they were to be informed by the same principles of liberty, equality and harmony that were the essence of the Revolution. In short, the remaking of the family was to be the French Revolution writ small. It was, however, a policy of no small importance, for there was a belief that the experiences of family life conditioned and prepared men and women for life in society and the polity at large. Celibates, men who refused to participate in family life, were condemned as dangerously antisocial, and even (by some) as counterrevolutionary. When the Year III (1795) version of the Declaration of Rights and Duties of Man and the Citizen declared that "no man is a good citizen if he is not a good son, a good father, a good brother, a good friend, a good husband,"[3] it did no more than state the intimate relationship between family and state, and family and Revolution, that had informed family law and policy for the preceding six years.

These, at least, were the plans of many revolutionaries. But they realized that new relationships could not simply be prescribed and then imposed on the population. By enacting new family legislation such as that requiring equality of inheritance, they created the structures for more equality and harmony within families: when daughters and younger sons were able to inherit in equal measure, the terrible rivalries and conflicts engendered by inequality under the Old Regime would wither away. The process would be hastened as French women and men were regularly reminded of the benefits of equality and harmony. Participation in the Festivals of Marriage would reinforce the message. The government would do all it could to regenerate the family, this most important of institutions, by legislating, prescribing, and exhorting. At that point the task was turned over to the people: men and women, children, parents, and siblings were expected to purify their attitudes and behavior of the poisons with which they had been contaminated under the Old Regime.

The question is, then, how the provinces responded to these policies that emanated from Paris. It is important that we should not think of the dichotomy between Paris and the provinces in narrowly geographical terms, such that Paris becomes seen as an island of Revolution in a turbulent ocean of counterrevolution. In such matters as the reception of the new family laws and policies, the legislators were Paris and the people at large were the provinces. What we should want to know is whether the family laws and policies were welcomed, obeyed, ignored, or resisted, and what patterns of compliance and noncompliance may be detected.

We should admit immediately that the attempt to regenerate the family (in the revolutionaries' sense) failed. There is no evidence of wholesale shifts in attitudes or interpersonal behavior during the revolutionary decade, and that is no more than we should expect.[4] It might have been possible to create new political institutions or reconstruct old ones in a short period, but it was clearly unrealistic to expect to transform such a fundamental institution and network of relationships as the family within the same timespan. It might well be, as some historians have suggested, that the Revolution created the bases for the transformation of the French family,[5] but the process of change is scarcely perceptible during the Revolution itself. What is evident, however, is that the new family policies met with a varied response among the people. Some of the innovations were welcomed, others were accepted; some were simply ignored, while yet others were actively resisted. If nothing else, the story of the revolutionary attempt to remake the French family indicates another area in which the limits of the Revolution may be defined.

One set of limits was established by the very servants of the Revolution, the tens of thousands of functionaries, officials, registrars, justices, and judges throughout France whose job it was to see that the new laws and policies (family and otherwise) were applied and observed. In far too many cases these officials themselves subverted the effectiveness of policies by simple ignorance, incompetence, or laziness. That was bad enough, but in other cases officials deliberately acted in such a way as to frustrate the purpose of the new legislation.

It was to be expected that the transition from old to new practices would cause confusion among officials and ordinary citizens alike. Some confusion was generated when the Constitution of 1791 declared that marriage was nothing more than a civil contract, and that the means of determining and recording civil status would be established.[6] The constitution was promulgated in September, 1791, but it was not until September of the following year that a law created civil registers of vital events, made provision for civil marriage, and legalized divorce.[7] In the intervening twelve months, matrimonial confusion reigned. In various parts of France, couples interpreted the article on marriage in the constitution as meaning that they could marry civilly. Others, already married, concluded that if marriage was no more than a civil contract, they could break it and divorce. Such couples were abetted in their misinterpretations of law by various officials, and in many parts of the country, mayors, municipal councils, justices of the peace, and judges joined some couples and divorced others, even though they had no authority whatsoever to do so. A number were sufficiently anxious about their actions to write to the Legislative Assembly, announcing civil marriages and divorces, and urging the legislators to make legal provision for such acts.

In the end these marriages and divorces were retroactively validated, but in the short term they placed couples in potentially difficult positions. In some cases the officials must simply have misunderstood the meaning of the article in the 1791 constitution. It was, after all, France's first constitution, and might have been thought to be a statute. Others probably acted on the naive assumption that a declaration of principle was tantamount to a law. In yet other instances the illegal marriages and divorces could have rested on nothing more sinister than ignorance of law and procedure. When divorce was finally legalized in 1792, "a crowd" of priests wrote to the bishop of Rouen, in Normandy, asking what their attitude to divorce should be.[8] If priests were unsure of the canon law of marriage, it should hardly be surprising to find officeholders, many of them carrying out their responsibilities for only a short time, uncertain as to the extent of their authority and the precise implications of the constitution.

Other officials, however, performed their duties less than conscientiously, and incurred the anger of the central authority. The *état civil*, registers of civil status that recorded births, marriages, divorces, and deaths (and sometimes legitimations and adoptions), were viewed as the infrastructure of the new family system. The Old Regime equivalent of the *état civil* was the parish registers kept by the Catholic church, although they were used to record the sacraments of baptism, marriage, and burial, rather than specifically vital events. Even so, the civil authorities of the Old Regime had attempted to see that registers were kept properly, although from time to time there were conflicts between church and state on the issue. As historians who have used the Old Regime parish registers know only too well, the completeness of information they contain varied not only from place to place, but from priest to priest; some were more diligent than others, while some were so overworked that their registrations were permanently in arrears.

Anxious to avoid the problems that all too often had undermined the usefulness of the parish registers, the revolutionary authorities provided full and clear instructions as to what the registration of each birth, each marriage, each divorce, and each death ought to include. Later in the Revolution, forms were supplied, so that the registrars had only to fill in such information as names, occupations, addresses, and so on. Such evident concern for proper and full documentation was not simply a case of bureaucrats wanting rules followed for the sake of following rules. As a circular from the Ministry of the Interior observed in the Year V (1797): "The tranquility of families rests, Citizens, on the accuracy of the *état civil* of citizens; the matter is of such great importance that it cannot be given too much attention by the government."[9] The *état civil* was the means by which marriages would be verified, for example, and on marriage depended such fundamentally important issues as legitimacy and the rights of inheritance. The information in the *état civil*, in short, would be the raw material for the determination of rights in the new family system.

In the meantime, however, there were problems in the provinces, as careless *officiers publics* (civil registrars) undermined the *état civil*. Although the civil registers were generally well kept, problems were discovered in certain areas. In the Year III (1795) the administrators of the department of Côte-d'Or, in eastern France, surveyed the *état civil* in the area around Dijon and were appalled at their findings. In the commune of Saulon-la-rue they found that the wording in the death registers "is not French," and that there was no index to the registry of deaths.[10] In Chevrey, the first entry in the registry of deaths was so marked by erasures that the name of the deceased was quite illegible, and in the records of marriages, entries were so often obscured by erasures and corrections that their meaning was lost.[11] In the commune of Layer, the administrators noted, "in general the registers . . . are very poorly kept, are not written correctly, and employ terms that have been abolished, such as godfather and godmother."[12]

Ignorance of the law was one thing, and carelessness in keeping records was another. Obstruction of the intent of the law was an offense of a quite different order, however. One example emanated from the commune of Mesnil-Raoult, near Rouen, in 1793. In March of that year Marie Aubery started divorce proceedings (for reason of incompatibility) against her husband Gilles Romé, who was mayor of the commune. The divorce had to be obtained in Mesnil-Raoult because that was where they had last lived together, even though Marie Aubery had gone to live with her father in Rouen. However, she returned to Mesnil-Raoult on April 18, 1793, to attend the family court in the municipal offices, only to be told that she had to wait. After she had waited for an hour, her husband and six municipal officials, all adorned in tricolored sashes of office, presented themselves, and informed her that the municipal council had just met to discuss matters, and had decided that she was not entitled to a divorce. Furthermore, it ordered her to return to her husband's dwelling, and although she attempted to escape so as to go back to Rouen, she was forced to go to Romé's house.[13]

Aubery made her getaway soon afterwards, however, and immediately appealed her husband's action to the district court in Rouen.

Romé did not deny what he had done, but justified his behavior by his desire "to make his wife return to the midst of her children so that she might rediscover the feelings that some men, who are keeping her far from her husband and family, are trying to extinguish." Besides, he said, he believed "that his wife does not enjoy all the freedom that she must have in order to understand the importance of the step she is taking, and that the only place where she will be in a condition to judge it properly is in her husband's house and among her children."[14]

The district court declared that Romé's attitude and actions were an attack on Aubery's rights. It held that the municipal council of Mesnil-Raoult had no competence to act as it had done, forbade Romé "to attack the freedom of his wife," and authorized her to live with her father in Rouen while pursuing the divorce. Even so, Romé continued to attempt to obstruct the divorce by formally opposing the final decree that was issued in the Year II, and again he was overruled by the court.[15]

A different set of circumstances, but a similar abuse of local authority, came to the attention of the Commission du Pouvoir Exécutif of Côte d'Or in the Year VII (1798). It concerned the birth of a child several years earlier, in the rural community of Villotte. According to the registers of the local administration, on September 18, 1795, Marthe Bouy, a midwife, reported to Claude Prudon, the local registrar, that one Catherine de Vigne had given birth to a child. Asked who the father was, Bouy was unwilling or unable to tell him. At this point, "Prudon, the public registrar, thought about matters for two or three hours and read the text of the law [of September 20, 1792, on the *état civil*], and having read through the law, he observed that Article seven of it required the surnames and first names of the father and mother before a registration of birth could be made in conformity with the law, and that without knowing the surname and name of the father of the child whose birth the midwife had announced, he could not register the birth. . . ."[16] The next day Prudon visited Jean Marchand, the mayor of Villotte, "and said to him, 'Citizen mayor, we must try to discover the identity of the father of the child of which the midwife made the declaration. As we know who the mother is, let us find out the identity of the father right away.'"[17]

A veritable posse, composed of the mayor, the registrar, and several other local officials, promptly made its way to Catherine de Vigne's dwelling, where she was found lighting the fire. "Who is the father of the child that you have brought into the world?" they demanded. "She replied, 'It is my brother in law,' to which . . . Lamas [a municipal official] responded 'Tell us who your brother in law is,' and the said de Vigne declared, 'It is Pierre d'Ecoulougue.'"[18]

Once the mystery had been cleared up, the registrar made an entry in his *état civil*, noting that the midwife (herself married to a Louis d'Ecoulougue—yet another brother, perhaps—which probably accounted for her initial reluctance to be more helpful) had reported the birth of a female child, and that the mother had declared that the father was not Jean d'Ecoulougue, her husband, but her husband's brother, Pierre.[19]

These two apparently minor incidents, the attempt by Gilles Romé, the mayor of Mesnil-Raoult, to prevent his wife, Marie Aubery, from divorcing him, and the inquiry into the paternity of Catherine de Vigne's baby in Villotte, exemplify both the persistence of traditional attitudes toward women, and the misuse of official authority to thwart the new policies that improved women's lot in private life. Under the Old Regime, divorce had not been possible, and it was a legal principle that a woman had to reside with her husband unless she was authorized by a court to live separately.[20] The actions of Marie Aubery's husband in attempting to block her divorce and forcing her to return home were in keeping with the principles of the Old Regime. Similarly the investigation into the identity of the man who had fathered Catherine de Vigne's child smacked of earlier times. Under the Old Regime unmarried women who became pregnant were required to make a *déclaration de grossesse* (a declaration of pregnancy), and if this declaration did not identify the father, the midwife who attended the birth was required to elicit the information for the authorities. With the coming of the Revolution, however, declarations of pregnancy were suppressed, inquiries into paternity were forbidden, and it became a principle of civil law that the father of a child born to a married woman was her husband.[21]

These cases and others like them suggest the ways in which officials not only failed to apply the new family laws, but followed procedures more in keeping with the very Old Regime codes and values that were condemned by the revolutionary legislators and policymakers as corrupt and unjust. Nor were officials in small rural communities the only offenders, although they might have had a better chance of escaping official attention. The judges in the city of Rouen interpreted some revolutionary laws in a distinctly prerevolutionary fashion when it came to cases of marital violence.

One of the legal reforms made early in the Revolution was a law on assault that provided severe penalties against men who assaulted women. A man convicted of assaulting another man could be fined five hundred *livres* and imprisoned for six months, but a man who assaulted a woman faced twice the fine and double the period in prison. This was a departure from Old Regime law, under which a man could beat a woman with impunity, as long as he did so "moderately," and she was his wife. All over France women attempted to invoke the new law to prosecute their husbands for having assaulted them.[22]

In practice, however, judges could be quite inconsistent in dealing with such prosecutions, as a number of cases in Rouen demonstrate. In one case the judges dealt severely with a husband who, his wife had alleged, "struck her several blows, kicked her several times when she was preparing to come into the house, and since throwing her out of the house has ceaselessly insulted her." The husband was ordered to pay damages of a thousand *livres*, a fine of a hundred *livres*, and was imprisoned for two weeks.[23] In other, apparently similar, cases, however, the court simply refused to accept jurisdiction on the grounds, as it was expressed to one plaintiff, "that this is simply a matter of a dispute between a husband and a wife."[24] In several cases, indeed, the court explicitly upheld the husband's authority over his wife, and implicitly defended his right to beat her. Commenting on the case of one Marie Mansele, the judges held that "seeing that [she] . . . is under the authority of her husband, that she is not divorced, and that she has not yet taken steps to obtain a divorce, the court declares that at present she is not entitled to bring this action against her husband."[25] How many divorces such judgments might have set in action we do not know, but within a week of the court's decision Marie Mansele had started divorce proceedings against her husband for reason of ill-treatment.

Similarly, a frustrated legal action against her husband led indirectly to the divorce of Marie Tavernier in Rouen. Her action against her husband for assault was rejected by the court, and she was advised "to take whatever action seemed appropriate," a broad hint, given that her prosecution was denied because "she is not divorced from her husband, and she is under his authority until she has started proceedings and they have been dealt with."[26] Tavernier's husband took informal action to end the marriage, however, by deserting his wife almost immediately. She divorced him in 1800 on the grounds of his absence for five years.[27]

Historically, the reluctance of the courts to intervene in matrimonial disputes is common enough, but during the Revolution the law did give women some protection from their husbands' violence. Under the Old Regime women had lived under the principle of *puissance maritale* (the husband's authority), and, as indicated, husbands had possessed the right to beat their wives providing they did so "moderately." This principle was eliminated from the revolutionary family codes. Nonetheless, persistent enunciation of it by the judges in Rouen, together with their refusal to accept jurisdiction in many such cases, testifies to a commitment to patterns of male dominance within marriage that were at odds with revolutionary law and ideology.

Such examples show how registrars, municipal officials, and judges could undermine the effectiveness of revolutionary laws and policies by interpreting them in the light of old practices, or by simply ignoring them. But the people themselves, who were to be the beneficiaries of the policies of equality and liberty, also had a habit of subverting them in various ways. In some localities people insisted on being married by the local priest, sometimes a priest in hiding who ministered clandestinely, rather than by the mayor. And they preferred to have their nuptials recorded on parish registers that, after 1792, had no legal value, rather than on the *état civil*. Claude Marre, priest in the parish of Montaut (Ariège), kept clandestine registers of baptisms, marriages, and burials throughout the Revolution, and a comparison of them with the local *état civil* allows us to see what use was made of the respective registers.[28]

As far as marriages were concerned, most people tried to satisfy both state and church: between 1793 and 1801, fifty-seven percent of couples in Montaut underwent a civil ceremony over which the mayor presided, as well as a religious ceremony conducted by the priest. On the other hand, thirty-three percent of couples marrying during the Revolution chose to have only a religious celebration, while a mere ten percent opted for the civil ceremony alone. The overwhelming preference for a wedding according to Catholic, rather than republican rites, is reinforced by the fact that two-thirds of the couples who chose both forms of marriage had their marriages celebrated first by the priest, and only later by the mayor. Indeed, in many cases the civil marriage followed by months or years, suggesting that the prime concern of some couples might have been to ensure that their children were legitimate in the eyes of the law.

The law on the *état civil* of September 20, 1792, required all births, marriages, divorces, and deaths to be recorded on the civil registers. It was a contentious law, not least because baptisms, marriages, and burials, which could no longer be recorded by the church, were sacraments and, in the minds of the faithful, the sacraments were vital to salvation. Failure to baptise a child was a sin, and failure to be married by a priest meant that one was not married at all in the eyes of God. It was clear from the very beginning that the *état civil* would meet some resistance.

A month after the law of September 20 was passed, the episcopal council of Côte d'Or alerted priests that the new system endangered the faithful, who might be led into error by "ill-intentioned people." In a pamphlet, the council enjoined the clergy to perform baptisms, marriages, and burials, and to maintain parish registers in duplicate, with one copy to be sent to the civil authorities.[29] Two weeks later, Côte d'Or department officials warned of the "dangers of distributing" this pamphlet, and instructed the bishop of Côte d'Or to send them a copy without delay.[30] The bishop complied, but pointed out that he had not been present when the resolution was passed. The officials promptly warned Paris that the pamphlet "was already causing alarm among the citizens." The law of September 20 was not intended to infringe on the freedom of citizens to have births, marriages, and deaths *sanctified* by religious ceremonies, but ministers of religion were not authorized to keep registers of these events.[31]

How widely this law was contravened, as men and women resorted first or solely to priests for baptisms, marriages, and burials, cannot be known for certain. A priest could continue to administer and record the sacraments only when he had a sympathetic and protective host community, so we should expect these illegal registers to turn up in the more devout regions. For the same reason we should expect the priest's services to have been well patronized. Even when priests were legally able to say masses and carry out their other pastoral duties, the civil authorities took a dim view of their attempting to perform functions (like celebrating marriages) that the state had taken over. In 1793 the administrators of Côte d'Or learned that citizen Mochot, the priest in the village of Gemeaux, had announced the banns of a marriage at mass on September 8, and had "invited those who knew of any impediments to the marriage to come forward." The administration in Dijon wrote that "far from restricting himself to purely ecclesiastical functions . . . citizen Mochot has carried out civil functions, by publishing a marriage bann, and has tried to make himself judge of the impediments that might prevent this marriage."[32] Should he persist in this behavior, he would be deprived of his salary, and might even be prosecuted. A notice to this effect was printed and ordered to be displayed in every commune in the department.[33]

Three years later the administration in Dijon found itself pursuing this matter again, this time because there had been complaints of priests keeping baptismal registers. The commissioner of the department wrote to the Minister of the Interior that "people in the countryside are exempting themselves from having births registered by the civil registrar." The priests who were keeping the illegal registers were "difficult to find," but, he insisted, it was important to provide severe penalties against ministers of religion who baptised any child."[34] In reply, the ministry wrote that the abuses complained of "may be easily curbed": the officials of each canton should be told to watch for any father, or other person, who failed to register a newborn child on the *état civil*, and to prosecute him or her vigorously under the terms of the law that specified two months' imprisonment for the offense. Such abuses would cease, the ministry concluded, if public officials were "more precise and more severe in their enforcement of the laws."[35]

At least the *état civil* faced no competition from the parish registers in the matter of divorce. But although divorce was anathema to Catholic marriage doctrine, French men and women, in the urban centers especially, appear to have welcomed or accepted it. This tendency represents a reversal of the persistence of Catholic practices in the rural areas, and speaks to a fundamental division between town and country. The general picture of divorce has been documented by many local studies,[36] all of which tend to confirm that divorce in the

French Revolution had two main characteristics: it was above all urban, and it was used more frequently by women than by men.

The statistics of divorce in and around Rouen and Dijon provide
examples of these traits. Under the terms of the very liberal divorce
law of 1792 (which was in effect until 1803) there were 1,046 divorces
in Rouen and 118 in Dijon. If we exclude the divorces by mutual consent and consider only those divorces sought by one spouse or the other,
we find that women sought exactly the same proportion in each town:
seventy-one percent.[37] Moreover, the incidence of divorce declined in
the rural areas. In the communes around Rouen and in the smaller
urban centers of the department of Seine-Inférieure, there were few
divorces. The canton of Mont-aux-Malades that surrounded Rouen had
a population of about 12,500, compared to Rouen's 85,000. But whereas
the city produced 1,046 divorces, the canton produced only 31.[38] Divorces, then, were in the ratio 1:38, although population was in the
ratio 1:7. Expressed crudely in relation to population, divorces were
five times more common in Rouen than in the adjacent countryside.[39]
The same tendency has been illustrated in the areas around cities such
as Toulouse, Metz, and Lyon.[40]

What do patterns of divorce tell us about the reception of this particular family law in the provinces? We should first attempt to understand why divorce was consistently less popular in the rural areas than
in the large towns and cities. Was it simply that the people of the countryside were more devout, more faithful than their worldly and secu-
larizing urban cousins to the doctrines of the Catholic church? No doubt
there is something to be said for this, but there appear to have been
critical social and economic factors also at work in the urban-rural
differences in divorce behavior.

The ability to avail oneself of the divorce law meant being able
to live and work independently, and this was more likely to be possible in a city than in the countryside. Towns offered casual accom-
modation and a labor market, albeit limited, whereas the rural economy was essentially familial: men and women lived and worked as
marital or family units. To this extent men and women, but especially
women, were locked into a family economy in the countryside, such
that divorcing meant not only leaving one's spouse, but also, in all
likelihood, leaving the locality for an urban center.

This, indeed, was the pattern in divorces in the rural districts around Rouen. Divorces were not only fewer there, but instead of being dominated by women, as they were in Rouen and other towns, they were dominated by men. Men, who lodged only twenty-nine percent of the unilateral divorce petitions in Rouen, were responsible for precisely twice that proportion, fifty-eight percent, in the rural areas around the city. Women, it seems, did not have the same ability to initiate divorce in the country as they did in town. Moreover, and as if to illustrate the difficulties faced by a divorced woman in a rural area, most of the women who divorced in the canton around Rouen migrated to the city, where they found employment in the textile industries.[41]

What this analysis suggests is that the pattern of divorce was influenced not only by ideological considerations (which must have been important) but also by the material conditions of marriage for the mass of the eighteenth-century French population. The population distribution of France was primarily rural, and its economic organizations was primarily familial. Married men and women were, for the most part, bound to each other by the ties of economic interdependence. Women whose husbands had deserted them were free of marital constraints, and could divorce easily. But others had to have an independent income or source of survival before they could countenance divorce. Perhaps that is why so many divorce actions were abandoned before being completed. In Rouen between 1792 and 1803 at least thirty-five percent of the divorce actions that were begun were withdrawn by the petitioners in the course of proceedings.[42] What this means is that if the intentions of the revolutionary legislators were to make divorce easily, cheaply, and speedily available to men and women who had good reason to want to escape their marriages, they did all they could in terms of the law and its institutions. But they could do nothing to compensate for the material constraints that impinged particularly on rural women, who could not have used divorce even if they had wanted to. To this extent, the liberty to divorce, apparently offered to all women and men equally, ran aground on the material realities of the eighteenth-century family.

This is not to say that divorce was universally welcomed in principle, if difficult to use in practice. It was generally condemned by the church, and we can assume that it had no great appeal to the mass of the faithful, even if there is no coherent historical record of their opposition. Men and women adversely affected by divorce did, however, voice their complaints. One was a citizen Genise of Rouen, who was moved to write thus to the Convention in 1795: "The pitiful victim of an abuse sanctioned by the law, crying tears of blood and with my heart broken with sadness, in the name of suffering and ceaselessly outraged humanity, I implore the assistance of your sense of justice and the influence you have in the Convention, to change the law of divorce, an unspeakably barbarous law that strikes one of the most severe blows to the common happiness and which ravages most families which would have been harmonious and peaceful were it not for its existence. . . ."[43]

Genise explained that after seventeen years of happy married life he had been imprisoned, only to discover, upon his release, that his wife was divorcing him for reason of incompatibility. After the divorce he remarried and (he said) gave his new wife everything, including new clothes for the wedding. But she was not grateful, and "constantly threatens me with divorce if I do not satisfy all her whims or when I allow myself to make the slightest representation to her."[44] Genise concluded this tale of matrimonial woe by begging the legislators to abolish divorce.

But if citizen Genise thought divorce unjust and harmful, there were thousands of men and women (mostly women) who found it a benefit. It enabled some to escape from oppressive and violent marriages, and it enabled others to give legal form to the termination of a marriage that had ended by desertion, absence, or de facto separation many years before. One case in Rouen was particularly revealing. Edme Hérard, a disabled military officer, and Anne Barrouin, his wife, appeared before the registrar of vital statistics and explained that "not having seen each other for ten years or thereabouts, having no fixed domicile and having run into each other quite by chance in this town, they came to the district court . . . in order to get permission to divorce by mutual consent."[45] In another case, one of Rouen's first, Marie Piedeleu divorced her husband in December, 1793; she had last seen him when he left to serve in the Seven Years' War, in 1757, thirty-six years earlier. To such people, divorce was a formality, but it gave legal form to their marital status and permitted them to remarry.

Not only did those immediately involved in divorces appear to accept it without qualms, but so did their friends and relatives who acted as witnesses before the courts, arbiters in court proceedings, and co-signatories on the divorce registrations in the *état civil*. Each divorce necessarily drew in at least another five individuals, and one must assume that they would not have participated in the process if they had had severe reservations about the moral legitimacy of divorce. Witnesses to the facts were a separate category, of course, for they could be involved despite themselves; one witness in a Rouen divorce case was a refractory priest.

For all that we have noted opposition to aspects of the new family policies, indeed, we find acceptance of them in an apparently willing compliance with the laws. While some parents insisted on having their children baptised, and some couples boycotted the civil ceremony of marriage, most observed the new forms. All over France, in fact, couples married in record numbers and had their marriages recorded in the *état civil*, even if some also had a religious ceremony. Not only that, but once they could marry without the participation of the clergy, they quickly ignored the periods of penance (Lent and Advent, notably) when marriage was prohibited by the church.[46] Overall, the French population appeared to accept the forms set down by the law, and in the cities and towns even innovations like divorce proved acceptable.

It is an open question how noncompliance ought to be regarded. The revolutionary authorities treated it as criminal, but not necessarily counterrevolutionary. Areas of extensive noncompliance with the law of the *état civil* might well have been areas where opposition to the Revolution was extensive, but in itself the preference for a priest over the civil registrar can be explained more satisfactorily in terms of tradition than as an explicitly counterrevolutionary act. Secularization of marriage, legalization of divorce, and creation of the *état civil* were certainly important parts of the work of the revolutionaries in remaking the family, and they were certainly challenges to the practices of Catholics. But for the mass of the population, these innovations in family law appeared to arouse relatively little contention.

It was not so with inheritance, however. Under the Old Regime inheritance laws and practices had varied a great deal, but most codes had embodied inequalities, as the rules favored one child over the others or males over females. Early in the Revolution the rule of male primogeniture was abolished for noble families, partly to force nobles to divide their estates equally among all heirs at each generation, and thus progressively to destroy noble fortunes. Immediately, however, there were demands that the new rule of equal inheritance by all children should be applied universally. Arguments were framed in terms of both principle and pragmatism. Unequal laws of inheritance set not only children against parents, but siblings against siblings, it was argued, and the results—"bitterness, jealousy, and often misery"[47]— were depicted as having serious social and political implications. A petition from a group calling itself "the Paris Society of Friends of Harmony and Equality within Families" insisted that many younger children, "victims of wicked laws, or of the despotism of wicked parents," had been unable to marry because they were deprived of their rightful inheritance. Inequality of inheritance, the society wrote, "has depraved every character; each citizen has been corrupted in the cradle; he has drunk, with his mother's milk, meanness and selfishness: is it surprising, after that, that for so long in France there has been nothing but slavery? Our primogeniture snuffed out our virtues."[48] The language employed was clearly political, and stressed the familial source of civic virtue. It is resonant of declarations by revolutionary women that their children would drink the pure milk of liberty from their breasts.[49]

Children who benefited from unequal inheritance laws were not spared the trenchant criticism often directed at despotic parents. There were petitions from women in Normandy seeking redress against inheritance practices that had excluded them and that had made their brothers "little tyrants."[50] Elsewhere younger sons, also excluded from succession, used a political analogy in their call for the abolition of primogeniture to be applied retroactively in order to deprive eldest sons of the benefits they had derived from privilege: "younger sons [cadets] in the family dwelling are like the people [le peuple] in a state; if the heir should be deprived of his empire, should he evoke more pity than a tyrant who loses his throne?"[51]

There was even a suggestion that older brothers were likely to be influenced by their selfish material interests to oppose not only the reform of inheritance law, but the revolution of justice and equality in general. A petition of the Year II (1793–94) praised the revolutionary legislators for having destroyed a system that gave the firstborn son "all the wealth and affection of his father and condemned his brothers to the most appalling misery . . . made of the former a domestic tyrant, and of the latter vassals, valets or serfs. . . ."[52] The petition suggested that the rigorously unequal inheritance laws in the south of France under the Old Regime had led younger, disinherited children there to rally to the Revolution, despite attempts by their elder brothers to frustrate them. "If the southern parts of this land have offered so many defenders to the state, it is because, having within their laws yet another enemy to fight, they have had to make even greater efforts."[53] The petition pressed the point that "younger sons have served the Revolution best," and ended: "the wisdom that has presided over the pacification of the Vendée, may, in a word, bring peace and happiness into the hearts of families, bring brothers together, and forge from civil and political equality the bond that must unite them for ever."[54] Here was an appeal for fraternity in the most literal sense. It was an appeal to which the legislators responded with new, egalitarian, laws of succession.

Yet family harmony and cooperation, virtues and qualities promoted by the Revolution, proved elusive. It is entirely possible, in fact, that the revolutionaries misjudged the familial sentiments of the people when they elaborated their family policies. Although associations were made among family, society, and polity, many revolutionary policies were based upon a conception of the family as a limited domestic group. The stress on marriage and fertility, and on familial values of filial respect and parental obligation, evoked an image of what can almost be thought of as an isolated nuclear family household, largely insulated from external influences.

The notion that marital relationships and behavior within the family were private matters informed parts of the law of September 20, 1792. Under that legislation, divorce was permitted not only on specific grounds (such as adultery, violence, and desertion), but also by the mutual consent of both spouses and by reason of incompatibility of character and temperament. This last ground was provided explicitly so that a husband or wife would not have to reveal embarrassing details of married life: in such divorces no evidence needed to be provided. The ethic of privacy was extended to the institutions of divorce. Divorces sought by mutual consent, and divorce petitions based on alleged incompatibility, were to be presented to a family assembly (*assemblée de famille*) that was to consist of six relatives, three nominated by each spouse. If no (or not enough) relatives were available, friends and neighbors could be substituted for them. The task of the family assembly was simply to attempt to reconcile the spouses, and if reconciliation was not achieved after a specified number of attempts, the divorce took effect. Divorce petitions based on specific matrimonial faults or conditions (adultery, violence, desertion, and so on) were heard not by the family assemblies, however, but by family courts (*tribunaux de famille*). Again, the spouses were obliged to nominate relatives (or, if they were not available, friends and neighbors), but in these cases the task of the nominees was to judge the evidence and decide whether the divorce was justified.

The purpose of establishing family courts and assemblies composed of relatives of those involved in family litigation was not only to provide rapid and cheap disposition of cases (and easy access to divorce), but also to keep these family matters within the family. Yet this plan for intimate familial justice was subverted by those most concerned — the spouses involved in divorces and their relatives. As far as the family courts were concerned, less than a quarter (24 percent) of their members in Rouen between 1792 and 1796 were related to either spouse. Neighbors and friends made up almost half (46 percent), but the remaining thirty percent were lawyers, precisely the group that the legislators had tried to exclude when they established the family court.[55] As far as the family assemblies were concerned, however, the membership was rather different: thirty-six percent of their members in Rouen were relatives, sixty percent were friends and neighbors, and only four percent were lawyers.[56]

What these patterns make clear[57] is that the ideal — that family disputes should be resolved or disposed of judicially within the family — fell far short of realization. Petitioners for divorces on specific grounds preferred to nominate lawyers more often than relatives in many cases. In other instances, when a defendant spouse would not nominate members to a family court, members were nominated by the district court. Rather than go to the trouble of locating relatives, the district judges often named a lawyer, and in this way contributed to further undermining the familial content of the family courts.

Even when relatives were summoned to serve in the family courts or assemblies they often declined. If we take the divorces by mutual consent in Rouen, we find that 465 relatives were nominated to serve in family assemblies, but that only 327 (70 percent) actually appeared.

Some, it is true, had good reason, like the man who was in prison by order of the Committee of Public Safety. Most of the others, however, offered excuses that seem less convincing. One woman in Rouen, seeking a divorce for reason of incompatibility, named her father, a brother, and another relative to her team on the family assembly. None appeared: her father sent a message that "he did not want to come," her brother "could not come because one of his servants had gone mad, and had to be committed to the hospital" just when the family assembly was meeting, while the other relative declared that "he had hurt his leg."[58]

The frequent failure of men and women to nominate relatives, and the failure of so many nominated relatives to serve on the assemblies and courts, suggest that there was limited interest in the revolutionary ideal of intimate familial justice. Eventually, the legislators themselves became disillusioned with the experiment, and in 1796 they abolished the family courts (where family participation had been weakest and lawyers' participation strongest) and transferred divorces based on specific grounds to the regular courts. It seems likely that the family courts failed, in terms of the purpose for which they were established, because they were based on an illusion. The family was not the private, cohesive unit that was implied by the legislation, but was fractured along gender and generational lines, and was open to the scrutiny and, to some extent, the control of the community. This much was recognized by the provision that neighbors and friends might serve on the family courts, but only if relatives were not available. It is probable, however, that neighbors and friends were often more important in times of family conflict, particularly for women.[59]

The notion of private family life, as it was to develop during the nineteenth century, might well have been simply anachronistic during the Revolution as far as the mass of the people were concerned. How, then, did it come to underly some of the revolutionary institutions? We can only speculate, but it is at least possible that notions of privacy were gaining currency among the bourgeoisie, the class that dominated the revolutionary legislatures and which would embody the ideology of domesticity in the nineteenth century. It may be significant that those involved in divorces by mutual consent and for reason of incompatibility (where no evidence of marital faults or indiscretions needed to be made public) were of a generally higher social status than couples involved in divorces on specific grounds that had to be proved before a family court. Moreover, the first group had a higher representation (36 vs. 24 percent) of relatives among those who dealt with their divorces, and a much lower proportion of lawyers (4 vs. 30 percent). We might be able to discern in these statistics, in fact, a greater receptivity to familial justice by the bourgeoisie, and if that is so, the failure of the family courts might be explained in terms of class: the family-based institutions ill suited the community-oriented working class, members of which dominated the divorce lists in cities like Rouen.[60]

What conclusions are we justified in drawing, on the basis of these scattered examples, about the reception of family laws and policies during the Revolution? We should first note that there was no unanimity among the legislators themselves as to the wisdom of some of the reforms affecting the family. The *état civil*, the secularization of marriage, and the initial reforms of inheritance law were broadly accepted by successive regimes, however, and they proved generally acceptable, too, to the population at large. Other innovations, such as the legalization of divorce (particularly some forms of it, such as divorce for reason of incompatibility) were subjects of constant review and debate. Yet other reforms had short lives: the 1794 decree that made divorce a formality, and the law that granted equal rights of inheritance to illegitimate children, are examples. When we examine the practicalities of reforming the family during the Revolution, then, we are not faced with a coherent, consistent consensus even among the legislators gathered in Paris.

It is therefore hardly surprising to discover a range of attitudes and reactions in the provinces. For the most part, however, those elements of family law and policy that persisted through the Revolution and that impinged directly on all citizens were the least objectionable parts. It might have irked men and women in rural communities to have to report births and deaths to the local civil official, but this was only part of a more general shift of responsibilities from the church to the state. If divorce was offensive to the devout Catholics of the rural areas, they could at least console themselves that there was precious little of it in their communities; that it was common in the towns served only to reinforce rural attitudes toward city-dwellers.

As for social relationships within the family, it is impossible to gauge the effects of policy over such a short period of time as the Revolution occupied. The laws that reduced the authority and economic power of fathers and husbands might well have had an impact analogous to the decline of prestige of the church and nobility during the Revolution. No doubt the laws of marriage and divorce helped thousands of men and women, particularly women who were able to escape oppressive and unequal marriages. For the most part, however, the legal changes, for all that they embodied the spirit of liberty and equality and fraternity, could be reduced to nothing by the social and economic realities of family life. The revolutionary legislators were motivated by the best intentions as they set about remaking the French family in the image of the Revolution, but in the established behavior and attitudes of the people they met more than their match. In this sense the fate of social reform at the level of the family more or less reflected the fate of the Revolution itself.

NOTES

Some of the research for this essay was aided by a Fellowship at the Newberry Library, Chicago, and by a grant from Carleton University.

1. General works dealing with the family law of the Revolution are: Marcel Garaud, *La Révolution française et la famille* (Paris, 1978); Irene Thery and Christian Biet, eds., *La famille, la loi, l'état, de la Révolution au Code civil* (Paris, 1989); and *La Révolution et l'ordre juridique privé: rationalité ou scandale?* (2 vols., Paris, 1989), esp. I, 299–405. I am currently writing a legal, political, and social history of the family during the French Revolution. Tentatively titled *Family and Revolution*, it will be published by Cambridge University Press in 1992.

2. On the general issue of the relationships among political, ideological and legal change during the Old Regime and early part of the French Revolution, see Roderick Phillips, "Family and Political Ideology in Eighteenth-Century France," *Proceedings of the Annual Meeting of the Western Society for French History* 16 (1989): 361–68.

3. Article 4 of the Duties set down in the preamble to the Constitution of the Year III.

4. An important exception was the transformation of inheritance practices, as documented by Margaret Darrow in *Revolution in the House: Family, Class, and Inheritance in Southern France, 1775–1825* (Princeton, 1989).

5. See James F. Traer, *Marriage and the Family in Eighteenth-Century France* (Ithaca, 1980), and Jean Bart, "La famille bourgeoise, héritière de la Révolution?" in Marie-Françoise Lévy, ed., *L'enfant, la famille et la Révolution française* (Paris, 1990), 357–72.

6. Title II, Article 7 of the Constitution of 1791.

7. This was the law of September 20, 1792.

8. Jean-Baptiste Guillaume Gratien, *Lettre circulaire de J.-B. Gratien, évêque de Rouen, au clergé de son diocèse, sur l'administration des sacrements de baptême*

et de mariage (Paris, n.d. [October 19, 1792]), document in Archives départementales de la Seine-Maritime, Rouen (hereafter cited as AD Seine-Maritime).

9. Circular from the Ministry of the Interior, 7 Ventôse, An V (February 25, 1797), in Archives départementales de la Côte d'Or, Dijon (hereafter cited as AD Côte d'Or).

10. AD Côte d'Or, L1662, *état civil*, 21 Nivôse Year III (January 10, 1795).

11. Ibid.

12. AD Côte d'Or, L1662, *état civil*, 23 Brumaire Year III (November 13, 1794).

13. AD Seine-Maritime, LP 7132, Tribunal de District, April 20, 1793.

14. Ibid.

15. AD Seine-Maritime, LP 7143, Tribunal de District, 8 Prairial Year II (May 27, 1794).

16. AD Côte d'Or, L493, *état civil*.

17. Ibid.

18. Ibid.

19. AD Côte d'Or, *Etat civil* of Villotte, naissances, 1er jour complémentaire, Year III (September 17, 1795).

20. *Encyclopédie, ou dictionnaire raisonné des sciences, des arts et des métiers* (Neufchâtel, 1765), XV, 60.

21. Bart, "La famille bourgeoise," 370.

22. See Roderick Phillips, "Women and Family Breakdown in Eighteenth-Century France: Rouen 1780–1800," *Social History* 2 (1976): 197–218.

23. AD Seine-Maritime, LP 7716, Tribunal de Police Correctionnelle, 9 Floréal Year IV (April 28, 1796).

24. Ibid., 20 Prairial Year IV (June 17, 1796).

25. Ibid., 29 Brumaire Year V (November 19, 1796).

26. Ibid., 21 Brumaire Year IV (November 12, 1795).

27. AD Seine-Maritime, Etat-civil, Rouen: mariages et divorces, Year IX.

28. Suzanne Grezaud, "Un cas de registres paroissiaux tenus par un prêtre réfractaire," *Annales historiques de la Révolution française* 200 (1970): 346–49.

29. AD Côte d'Or, L492², *Extrait des Délibérations du Conseil épiscopal de la Côte d'Or* (Dijon, 1792).

30. AD Côte d'Or, L492². Letter of November 6, 1792.

31. AD Côte d'Or, L492², Letter from Directoire du Département, Dijon, to Ministre de Justice, Paris, n.d. [November 1792?].

32. Impediments to marriage, different from those set down in canon law, were established by the law of September 20, 1792.

33. AD Côte d'Or, L 492², *Arrêté du directoire du département de la Côte-d'Or, Qui fait défense au citoyen Mochot, ministre du culte catholique de Gemeaux, de contrevenir aux dispositions de la loi du 20 septembre 1792, relative au mode de constater l'état civil des citoyens.*

34. AD Côte d'Or, L 492, Letter from Commissaire du Directoire du Département de la Côte d'Or to Ministre de l'Intérieur, 9 Floréal Year IV (April 28, 1796).

35. AD Côte d'Or, L492², Letter from Pouvoir Exécutif, 24 Floréal Year IV (May 13, 1796).

36. See, for example: Jean Lhote, *Une anticipation sociale: le divorce à Metz et en Moselle sous la Révolution et l'Empire* (Metz, 1981); Roderick Phillips, *Family Breakdown in Late Eighteenth-Century France: Divorces in Rouen, 1792–1803* (Oxford, 1980); and Dominique Dessertine, *Divorcer à Lyon sous la Révolution et l'Empire* (Lyon, 1981).

37. There is an astonishing consistency among French towns in relation to the proportion of women petitioners. It was 71% in Rouen, 71% in Dijon, 71% in Nancy, 72% in Le Havre, and 73% in Metz. In Toulouse it was relatively low, at 64%.

38. AD Côte d'Or, Etat civil, Dijon: Mariages et Divorces, 1793–An XI (1803), *passim*.

39. See Phillips, *Family Breakdown*, 92–94.

40. See, for example, Simone Maraval, "L'introduction du divorce en Haute-Garonne: étude de moeurs révolutionnaires," (Mémoire de Diplôme d'Etudes Supérieures, Toulouse, 1951); Jean Lhote, "Le divorce à Metz sous la Révolution et l'Empire," *Annales de l'Est* 5ᵉ série, 3 (1952): 175–83; Dominique Dessertine, *Divorcer à Lyon*.

41. Phillips, *Family Breakdown*, 96–98. I have argued elsewhere that the material context of the family economy not only militated against informal separation and the use of divorce, but also affected definitions of marriage breakdown, by inducing in women (and men, though less so) flexible, and potentially very low, expectations of marriage. See Roderick Phillips, *Putting Asunder: A History of Divorce in Western Society* (Cambridge, 1988), 361–402.

42. Completed divorces were recorded in the *état civil*. The proceedings (such as a declaration by the petitioner of intent to commence an action) were recorded in the *Publications des promesses réciproques de mariages et des actes préliminaires de divorces*, of which there are 13 volumes covering the period November 1792–Brumaire Year XIII (with some gaps) in: AD Seine-Maritime, Etat-civil (divers).

43. Archives Nationales, Dᴵᴵᴵ 273, Comité de législation, pétitions: Seine-Inférieure, 19 Messidor Year III (July 7, 1795).

44. Ibid.

45. AD Seine-Maritime, Etat-civil (divers), Actes préliminaires de divorces, Division 1, April 9, 1793.

46. See Phillips, *Putting Asunder*, 223–25.

47. Newberry Library, Chicago (hereafter cited as NL), *Adresse d'un très grand nombre de Citoyens de la Commune et du District de Montélimar, Département de la Drôme, à la Convention nationale* (n.p., n.d.), 1.

48. NL, *Adresse présentée à l'Assemblée nationale, Pour demander, que l'égalité des partages, entre les enfans, soit rétablie* (Paris, n.d.), 4–5.

49. "We will suckle our children on the milk of purity to which we will add the natural and pleasing spirit of liberty." Address by the patriotic women of Clermont-Ferrand, *Archives parlementaires*, 1ère série, XXXVI, 172 (December 17, 1791).

50. NL, *Adresse des citoyennes de la ci-devant province de Normandie, département du Calvados, sur la loi du 17 Nivôse; à la Convention nationale* (Paris, n.d.), 5. Another petition was *Les Filles Mariées dans la ci-devant province de Normandie, au corps législatif* (n.p., n.d.).

51. NL, *Le dernier cri des cadets, à la Convention nationale* (Paris, n.d.), 6.

52. NL, *L'agonie de la loi du 17 Nivôse* (n.p., n.d.), 5.

53. Ibid.

54. Ibid., 16.

55. Information on the family courts in Rouen is from AD Seine-Maritime, LP 7096–7107 and LP 6760, *Tribunaux de famille*, 1792–An IV/1796. There is a discussion of these institutions in Roderick Phillips, "Tribunaux de famille et assemblées de famille à Rouen sous la Révolution," *Revue Historique de Droit Français et Etranger* 58 (1980), 69–79.

56. AD Seine-Maritime, Etat civil (divers), *Publications des promesses réciproques*. . . .

57. Similar trends have been noted elsewhere. See James F. Traer, "The French Family Court," *History* 196 (1974): 211–28.

58. AD Seine-Maritime, *Etat civil (divers), Promesses réciproques*. . . , 7 Nivôse, Year II (December 27, 1793).

59. See Roderick Phillips, "Gender Solidarities in Late Eighteenth-Century Urban France: The Example of Rouen," *Histoire sociale–Social History* 13 (1980): 325–37.

60. For an interpretation of the family courts, see Jacques Commaille, "Les tribunaux de famille sous la Révolution," in Robert Badinter, ed., *Une autre justice: contributions à l'histoire de la justice sous la Révolution* (Paris, 1989), 205–23.

"Speaking in the Name of the People": Joseph Fouché and the Politics of the Terror in Central France

CONCLUDING AN 1821 REPORT on harvests, the count de Busset, mayor of Busset in the central French department of the Allier, added the comment that since the French Revolution, most of the population of his village detested the bourgeoisie. In the same year, Maginnat, mayor of the Allier village of Vieure, ended his harvest report with the observation that the Revolution had produced an incurable gangrene among the sharecroppers of his village. The people of Vieure demonstrated so little respect for the law, according to the mayor, that it stunned local magistrates.[1]

Historians have had little difficulty explaining these comments: a deputy — Joseph Fouché — sent from Paris to the department in 1793, had launched a massive revolutionary campaign that had upset all traditional sense of deference.[2] As one historian explained sympathetically, Fouché came to the Allier and initiated a class struggle against the rich. He taxed local landowners and created people's armies to seek out enemies of the Revolution. He also replaced traditional religious symbols and holidays with Temples of Reason and Love, busts of Brutus, and utopian revolutionary festivals designed to promote egalitarianism and civic virtue. Others less sympathetic toward Fouché's contribution to the history of the Allier have emphasized his role in promoting the Terror and in the mass shooting of hundreds of political prisoners in Lyon. Still, all stress the significance of the outsider from Paris, an extreme radical, in encouraging local sharecroppers and workers to believe they had the power to make their own revolution.[3]

An analysis of Fouché's activities in the central French departments of the Allier and the Nièvre in late 1793 reveals a more complicated story. Elected as a moderate deputy from Nantes in 1792, Fouché only gradually turned toward the left in Paris. His radical politics combining social leveling, national defense, and secularization emerged in full flower only after he arrived in central France. His controversial dechristianization campaign only slowly spread to Paris, and then to the rest of France, ultimately culminating in Maximilien de Robespierre's reluctant introduction of the cult of the Supreme Being in late 1793.[4]

In contrast, the sharecroppers and day laborers of the Allier and the Nièvre had deliberately declared war on the bourgeoisie and grain merchants as early as 1789. They questioned the validity of a revolution grounded in the defense of private property. Through their actions they asserted the radical claim that national land and its fruits belonged to the community and not to the state. The right to labor, they suggested, included the right of the community to claim its share of the products of its labor, hence, the right to subsistence. Finally, at the outbreak of Revolution in 1789, they claimed religious space for themselves by dancing, eating, and drinking in their parish churches in defiance of their clergy. By the time Fouché arrived, people in the Allier and the Nièvre were already engaged in total revolution through social leveling, collecting "revolutionary" taxes, and challenging the content and the form of traditional Christianity by asserting the supremacy of their own carnivalesque Catholicism.[5] In short, one could as easily argue that Fouché was formed by his experience in central France as insist that the area was influenced by his presence.

This does not mean, however, that one can ignore the man. Earlier than most, Fouché recognized the implications of the revolutionary change taking place around him. After his mission to Nantes in March, 1793, he attributed counterrevolutionary risings to "ignorance and fanaticism."[6] In a declaration to the citizens of the department of the Aube in late June 1793, he described the triumph of "the People" of Paris over the Girondins with the following words: "The excess of oppression broke down through the restraints on the People's indignation. A terrible cry made itself heard in the midst of this great city. The tocsin and the cannon of alarm awakened their patriotism, announcing that liberty was in danger, that there was not a moment to spare. Suddenly the forty-eight sections armed themselves and were transformed into an army. This formidable colossus is standing, he marches, he advances, he moves like Hercules, traversing the Republic to exterminate this ferocious crusade that swore death to the People."[7] As historian Lynn Hunt explains, Fouché already understood that "'the People' is everywhere, but when it is assembled, when it comes together in a critical mass, it is transformed into a powerful new energy." Thus, "'the Terror' was a radical, emergency form of government," as well as "a real and disturbing experience for the men who supposedly invented it." Very vividly, Fouché describes the metamorphosis of individual wills into a new and frightening monster, the People. For Fouché, "the Terror was the People on the march, the exterminating Hercules."[8]

Comprehending the changes of 1793, Fouché symbolized his monster as Hercules. In mythology Hercules frequently killed others because of his excessive strength, often without being aware of what he was doing. When given challenging tasks, he accomplished them through brute force, not Reason. Thus, Fouché's account reveals an ambivalence about the source of his power, even before he began to exercise it decisively. In Hunt's words, Fouché's Hercules is not an intelligent monster, but "a mighty force, crying with the pain of betrayal, fierce when aroused; he reacts more like an injured animal than like an agent of his own destiny."[9] Hercules, in other words, needed the wise guidance of the People's representatives to provide them with Reason.

To endow the People with Reason, revolutionaries like Fouché created a new political culture. This culture depended upon revolutionary festivals to refashion men and women into secular revolutionary citizens. For historian Mona Ozouf, these festivals staged idealized versions of the utopia that revolutionaries like Fouché hoped their revolution would achieve.[10] But it can also be argued that they represented an attempt to tame the monster and to create men and women devoted to the deputies of the National Convention.

It is useful to examine Fouché's activities in central France for several reasons. Most important, his actions reflect the difficulty revolutionaries faced in 1793 in trying to create a political community out of atomized individual wills, prone to act on their own special interests. Moreover, by observing the interaction between Fouché and the people of the countryside, one can probe the process by which revolutionaries aimed to put into practice in provincial environments the rhetoric and discourse of the Revolution. Finally, by studying Fouché one can explore the fear inspired when the monster on its ferocious crusade acted collectively as the People.

By analyzing Fouché's activities in central France, one can also explore the implications of François Furet's argument that Hercules, the monster, the allegorical representation of the General Will, came to be more real during the Revolution than the phenomenon it represented. Whoever captured the political institutions and journalistic organs articulating this representation thus had the ability to speak, and hence to become "the word of the People." But, to maintain this status, revolutionaries had to define all opposition as a plot against the General Will, a process which resulted in the exercise of violence — the Terror — against anyone who challenged the government or its policies.[11]

Fouché attempted to put democracy into practice by "speaking in the name of the People." But his activities reveal a man caught up in an event — the Terror — that simultaneously brought to the masses both the possibility of political participation and an extreme authoritarianism, culminating in mass executions. At times, he was the incarnation of Dr. Frankenstein, the source of the monster himself.

Contradictions emerged when revolutionaries like Fouché, "speaking in the name of the People," carried the Revolution from Paris into provincial France. The revolutionary festivals and the Terror in the Allier and the Nièvre reveal the context within which his monster broke loose. They also reflect the struggle that revolutionaries had with the language and mythology of revolution when confronted with the special interests that they refused to acknowledge and attempted to obliterate. Fouché was not a serious political theorist, although in this period he appeared to have a well-articulated program. He added embellishments to official festivals that terrified even superiors like Robespierre. Nonetheless, he chose his symbols carefully from cultural and political resources available to him, particularly from the radical Hébertists. The effects of his festivals are confusing and contradictory. They demonstrate the difficulty of finding an appropriate cultural representation for the new democracy in the countryside of central France. In this region, the sharecroppers and day laborers were like Hercules: they cried with the pain of betrayal when revolutionaries defended the integrity of private property and became fierce when aroused into action to resist their enemies.

CENTRAL FRANCE ON THE EVE OF THE TERROR

The events of 1793 marked an important turning point for revolutionaries in Paris and, as a consequence, for those in rural France. Within months, the new republican government found itself at war with all of Europe. Early defeats cost France dearly. Attempts to conscript soldiers resulted in massive counterrevolutionary rebellion in the Vendée. As internal and external crises mounted, price rises in Paris induced popular committees to demand price controls on basic subsistence items. Eventually, the most radical elements in the National Convention, the Montagnards, consolidated their rule by agreeing to support the most extreme demands of the Parisian popular societies, including their demands to fix prices and to provide a greater supply of grain to major cities. After the Montagnards forcibly expelled recalcitrant moderates or Girondins from the Convention, Federalists in much of provincial France seceded from Parisian rule. By the summer of 1793, sixty-two of eighty-eight departments were in open revolt. To respond to these internal and external threats, the Convention first sent *commissaires* and then *représentants en mission* like Joseph Fouché to rural France.

The Convention wanted these deputies to fulfill three major objectives: (1) to raise an army, (2) to end counterrevolutionary and federalist tendencies, and (3) to aid poor *sans-culottes*, who formed the major social base of Montagnard support in Year II (August, 1793–August, 1794). Most used their missions to provide provincials with an elementary education in revolutionary politics. Nonetheless, although they were sent to impose republican unity, the individual representatives — each with his own personality and programs — constituted the real government of provincial France during the Terror.[12]

Peter Jones has argued that the deputies' "passage through the departments brought the Terror to the doorsteps of millions of country dwellers,"[13] but it is clear that they came to many parts of France where sharecroppers wanted to carry the Revolution much further than the radicals in Paris desired. Sharecropping was the predominant form of land tenure in perhaps as much as two-thirds of France.[14] In most cases, these sharecroppers barely eked out a subsistence living, often surrendering more than half of their harvest to landlords. In many parts of France, landlords simply incorporated the feudal dues eliminated in

1789 into lease payments demanded from sharecroppers. They also tended to lease farms to *fermiers généraux*, middlemen who would sublet holdings to sharecroppers. In many cases, their monopoly of holdings in specific villages allowed the *fermiers* to monopolize grain traded in commercial markets. In response to these conditions, sharecroppers gradually tried to make their own revolution by declaring war on the bourgeoisie and grain merchants.[15]

The worst violence emerged in the Allier and the Nièvre in 1790 when sharecroppers and day laborers took control of local government and excluded the bourgeoisie and grain merchants from political office. Armed peasants struggled with government forces for much of the year. Their most innocuous actions fixed the price of grain; their most dangerous threatened landowners' houses. They pillaged châteaux and claimed seigneurial forests as their own. Overwhelmed by force, the rural violence subsided for a year, then broke out again in 1792, when serious grain shortages developed.[16]

The violence in 1792 frequently involved claims that the property of émigrés and the church belonged to the community and not to the national government.[17] In Saint-Menoux in the Allier, for example, villagers claimed that the income from the sale of national lands belonged to the village rather than the state, since the value of the land was completely dependent on their labor.[18] Villagers were never legally able to assert their claims over national lands or forests, but through their practice of taking whatever they could carry, they often left the government with little movable property to sell. In the end, the national government had to create a special rural police force to protect forests and other properties claimed by the state.

Grain shortages worsened in 1793, bringing the local conflict to a head. To some extent, the shortages developed from poor harvests and bad weather. Contemporaries, however, often blamed landowners, who refused to plant grain in response both to rural violence and to new revolutionary laws that fixed prices so low that they reduced producers' profits.[19] Sharecroppers were hurt as much as others who depended on grain for their subsistence when landlords and *fermiers* insisted on sowing less.

In April 1793, the Popular Society of Nevers led by Socrates Damour entered the town of Clamecy in the Nièvre with the National Guard to reverse the effect of "seditious" priests. They spoke against the fanaticism of the rich and urged the population of Clamecy to make "war on the châteaux." They told men and women that it was time that they "ate white bread." Apparently, many agreed, and troubles continued to disrupt daily life in Clamecy until the arrival of Fouché in August.[20] On May 30, 1793, thirty citizens from Nevers urged vinegrowers in La Charité to take action against rich grain merchants. Riots continued in the town throughout the summer of 1793, as rural men and women pillaged the granaries of well-off merchants.[21]

More significant, often with the help of seditious priests, sharecroppers from central France began to petition the National Convention to end the abuses of sharecropping. Petitions came from several villages in the Nièvre, the Saône-et-Loire, and the Allier from 1790 until 1793. One petition called for the abolition of *fermiers* and grain merchants. Another threatened to destroy bourgeois property. Calling *fermiers* the "cancers of agriculture," the petitions demanded the elimination of *fermiers généraux*, the elimination of the practice wherein landlords could collect *dîmes* and other charges, and the division of harvests exactly in half. Most wanted to halt the practice of subletting and to eliminate the concentration of property in one landowner's hands.[22] In response, revolutionary officials tried to explain to sharecroppers in the Allier that landowners were still to be respected as property owners, even though they were no longer feudal lords.[23] In July 1793, officials in the Saône-et-Loire insisted that the laws abolishing feudal rights had no impact on sharecropping.[24]

The ambiguous economic position of the sharecroppers, however, renders any sharp characterization of their politics meaningless. In the fall, most sharecroppers had at least small surpluses they could market, even after surrendering at least half of their harvest. Since their sharecropping leases also required the payment of annual lease fees, their ability to continue to farm, in fact, depended on selling as much as they could. Like other producers, when they had crops to sell, they were against price controls. When their surpluses were expended, they joined other wage-earners in demanding lower market prices for grain.[25] Government grain policies, thus, could bring sharecroppers and landowners together in their capacity as grain producers, but only temporarily.

The Maximum, the law popularly associated with price-fixing, attempted to regulate the grain trade in its entirety. Passed on May 4,

1793, it not only fixed the price of grain, but also ordered proprietors, cultivators, and merchants to indicate how much grain they possessed, so that revolutionary officials could begin to make equitable requisitions of wheat and rye. Unable to survey grain because of armed opposition from landlords and grain merchants, officials in the Allier attempted to implement the Maximum anyway. On May 20, they published a list of official prices and demanded that parish priests read it at mass.[26]

The situation in the Allier was complicated by the fact that not all departments complied with the Maximum and even where they did, the Maximum set prices on the basis of departmental averages.[27] The adjacent and rebellious department of the Rhône-Loire, for example, refused to implement it, so grain merchants from Le Donjon and Cusset decided to ship their grain out of the Allier, where prices could rise. To stop them, on May 31, men and women halted grain shipments in the district of Chevagnes, forcing the merchants to sell them the grain at the Allier's fixed price. Other grain riots broke out throughout all of central France.

To stop trouble, Allier administrators forbade merchants to take their grain out of the department. Cantons and villages began to guard jealously everything they produced. Since some villages fixed prices lower than others, conflict multiplied. Grain consumers flocked to the villages where prices were low; grain producers wanted to sell only where prices were high. Over the summer, the Maximum lowered prices, although because of the decreasing amount of grain left at the end of the harvest year, prices naturally should have been rising. In this situation no one took grain to market. As the value of the Revolution's paper currency, the *assignat*, diminished, no one wanted to accept it in payment for grain. Instead, transactions took place in a black market economy housed deeply in the department's woods, away from the eyes of revolutionary agents.[28]

By July, convinced that only a huge army could force landowners and merchants to bring grain to market, Allier officials notified the Convention that it was abandoning the experiment. The scene was repeated in various forms elsewhere, and in Paris, the collapse of market regulation provided the background to the Montagnards' rise to power. Still, very little grain appeared for sale.

At the end of August, 1793, men working in the forest of Tronçais began to claim all grain for themselves. They invaded estates and took whatever they could in "the name of the People." They took grain that sharecroppers needed for seed and harvested crops themselves although they did not know how to use agricultural implements, therefore causing considerable waste. The department administration condemned this violation of private property and ordered manufacturers dependent upon wage labor to take responsibility for feeding their workers.[29] But employers could do nothing as long as grain growers brought nothing to market.

If grain problems were the most serious obstacles to revolution in the countryside, the opposition to conscription posed the most immediate threat to the National Convention, sitting in Paris. Without soldiers they had no hope of stopping foreign armies. In the *levée* of three hundred thousand men nationally, the Allier was to provide 2,975. Only a handful volunteered. When officials tried to draft rural men into the army, they faced massive revolts.[30] Although few of these riots were coordinated, as many as two hundred men armed with stones and clubs resisted conscription at Cosne in March, 1793, threatening to "slit the throats of all the bourgeoisie who make the laws."[31] In Laféline, armed sharecroppers refused to fight, arguing that "property owners themselves should defend their land."[32] Authorities put down the rebellions and arrested several forest workers, shoemakers (*sabotiers*), sharecroppers, and farm servants accused of fomenting revolt.[33] However minor, this collective refusal to join the army threatened revolutionary agents, who constantly feared the spread of the Vendée counterrevolution.[34]

But the sharecroppers of central France were not counterrevolutionary. Despite their actions, they seemed to be against the Revolution only when it benefited the bourgeoisie. Until autumn, 1793, revolutionary officials either ignored their protests or used force against them. This attitude changed with the arrival of Joseph Fouché.

"SPEAKING IN THE NAME OF THE PEOPLE": JOSEPH FOUCHÉ IN CENTRAL FRANCE

Naming the aristocrats, the religious, and the rich as his enemies, Fouché launched the official Terror in central France. Historians have argued that his war fundamentally changed the language and organization of local politics. They claim that he provided men and women with a new political vocabulary and taught them new tactics. But, except for his festivals, little of what he advocated was new. Local men and women were not necessarily moved by his ideas, for they had already acted them out.

Fouché's actions in the region seemed so bold to deputies in Paris that Robespierre questioned him in October. The deputy admitted that what would have been dangerous in other places would work among the sympathetic working population of central France.[35] He did not add that individuals and local revolutionary societies had already done such things before he had arrived. Nonetheless, although he spoke a language suitable to those he addressed, there can be no question of his efforts to mold the Revolution from above. This is particularly true of his festivals, which were aimed at teaching rural men and women the principles of revolution.

Fouché offered the key to his program in his first address to the people of the Nièvre on July 31. He argued that popular justice should be generous but not vengeful and reminded citizens of the new radical constitution of 1793. This constitution, he explained, put them in power. "I speak in the name of *your* personal interest," he added. "*The People do not need your support* to assure its triumph. It is the strongest of all powers on earth; the kings are finished; the People begin; their victory will crown its work, because it is unperishable; it is immortal like Divinity."[36] He defined the counterrevolutionaries of the Vendée and the federalists of Lyon as enemies of the People, who had outraged liberty.[37] They functioned as the raison d'être for his activities.

Already one can witness the ambiguity in revolutionary discourse. Fouché could with a good conscience tell his audience that he spoke in their name and then state that "the People do not need your support." He is at once acknowledging his power in speaking in the name of the People and illustrating how speech can substitute itself for power "as the sole guarantee that power belongs only to the People, that is to say to no one."[38] In the end, he could argue that he did not need the support of individuals as long as his speech was consistent with public opinion generally, although obviously his acceptance depended on public opinion; hence, on the People's support.

Fouché found supporters for his articulation of public opinion in both town and countryside.[39] In central France, he argued that wealth itself created dangerous conditions, hence it should be confiscated to promote the Revolution.[40] In both Clamecy and La Charité, he brought men and women together in festivals, where he explained to them that the rich were making them miserable. In these new festivals, he substituted civic virtue and social leveling for older religious ideas. "I spoke your language to them, explained your perceptions,"[41] he wrote to the Committee of Public Safety in Paris. In this letter, Fouché talks about "your" language, not the People's language. He thus seems to be making a distinction between his own language, the language of the People, and that of the Committee of Public Safety. This time, he seems to see public opinion coming from Paris, not from men and women in Clamecy and La Charité.

Like many deputies on mission, in one of his major acts in the Nièvre, Fouché organized a large civic festival on September 22 to inaugurate a bust of Brutus, a man who slew his best friend — Julius Caesar — and destroyed his family by slaying his sons to defend republican principles. This festival would mark "an epoch in the memory of free men," he wrote.[42] For him, it announced the end of superstition and the beginning of a new religion grounded in morality and a cult of virtue — one commensurate with the Constitution of 1793.

Critical to his festival was the exercise of terror. In the morning before a parade, he guillotined three "criminals" who had violated the laws of the Republic.[43] He wrote that it was necessary to execute these criminals "to strike terror at the beginning of the day" because it was only through terror that he could "prepare souls to most vividly feel *the sweet emotions of nature* and of *holy brotherhood.*"[44] The parade in the afternoon would make people understand the horror of the crime that destroyed sacred brotherhood.

In the parade, people danced and sang as Fouché led them into the city's now secularized cathedral. After placing the bust of Brutus on the altar, he introduced Anaxagoras Chaumette, a native of the Nièvre and a nominal leader of the Paris commune. Chaumette pointed out the difference between the morning's executions and the afternoon's procession. The executions destroyed the evil lurking in the Old Regime; the festival to Brutus inaugurated the new order.

As they do in a religious revival, men and women stood up and pledged to fight for the Republic. After the speeches, citizens prepared a banquet for the aged and infirm. Fouché and other officials served them, in a dramatic reversal of standard custom. This was a festival for the People, from whom all power derived; the government served them — especially the neediest — not the other way around. At the end of the day, men and women celebrated the new era by dancing in open air under a liberty tree.[45]

Except for the real executions, there is nothing remarkable in this particular festival. It was strictly ordered and everyone was given a part. Celebrating Brutus, however, was problematic. On the one hand, Brutus was the virtuous man who put safety of the state above private emotion. On the other, by destroying his family he undermined all legitimization of the private world of women. Women were brought into this festival, but the private correspondence of many women in France at the time indicated a conscious rejection of the "Roman fever" that employed a male personification of virtue. These women especially rejected Brutus, since his exercise of civic virtue depended upon obliterating and destroying the location of woman's virtue.[46] Thus, no matter how carefully Fouché (or others) tried to promote civic unity, divisions in society could not be obliterated in his festivals.

In this festival, Fouché used a real guillotine with real victims. The victims were unnamed; indeed, no one was told of their crimes. The executions were designed to differentiate the new virtuous citizens who promoted the public will from the subjects of the Old Regime who acted on their special interests against society. Both citizens and victims were faceless and nameless. The banquet — in which the government waited on the People — came closer to an allegorical statement, but even here, the minimal realism of a government deriving from the People seemed determined in advance. Fouché described the festival in utopian and poetic language linking the people of the Nièvre to the ancients, but it was, in fact, a clumsy effort that depended heavily upon his verbal explanations. He failed to mention in his official account that he also had two horses drag a cross in the mud and had two horsemen ride into the church following Chaumette. These carnivalesque gestures were almost certainly designed to please his local audience, not his superiors in Paris.[47]

A few days later, he moved to the Allier, where he promptly replaced the revolutionary government with men loyal to him.[48] He launched his first civic festival in Moulins on September 26, when he organized a mass procession to destroy the visible signs of the church. He began his festival from the cathedral, Nôtre-Dame. He now called himself the "apostle of liberty in the departments of the center and the west," who was in the Allier to "substitute for the superstitious and hypocritical cults to which people still unhappily cling, those of the Republic. . . ."[49]

This festival mixed his new religion with his attack on the rich. His brief civics lesson included a synopsis of the French Revolution: in the early stages it abolished nobility and clergy, now there were only oppressors and oppressed; the oppressors were speculators and hoarders, the oppressed, the mass of people. The Constitution of 1793 guaranteed everyone the right to eat, he stated, so that anyone who deprived people of that right was guilty of treason. Going further than he had in the Nièvre, he argued that the rich should no longer be allowed to use their wealth against the People, "but on the contrary, should be forced to divide up what is superfluous."[50]

Taking actions which anticipated national policy, Fouché declared that only one kind of bread —"equality bread"— would be sold. He fixed its price at three *sous*. Recognizing that this could hurt bakers, he demanded that the municipal council compensate the honest for lost profits. He also proposed creating philanthropic committees to "tax the rich in proportion to their number in a manner in which they would be able to pay for the labor of legitimate workers and provide subsistence for the honorable who had nothing." With one decree, he simply abolished poverty in the department.[51] He warned people of the enemies that true republicans faced and demanded that the department form a People's army. Popularizing clubs for youth, he urged them to supervise markets and declared that anyone who failed to cooperate with them "should have his head brought to the scaffold."[52] He followed his speech with an organized procession.

To encourage revolutionary fervor, Fouché fostered the development of committees of philanthropy and surveillance, which would sequester the property of émigrés. He encouraged People's armies to examine the homes of suspects and the rich to assure compliance with his laws. Sensitive to the complaints against *fermiers*, who many believed were refusing to plant because of the Maximum, he declared that the municipality should make sure that all land was seeded because "*sans-culottes* depend on this land."[53] He further demanded that rural areas bring requisitioned grain to market. Because merchants refused to accept *assignats* in payment, he ordered the People's armies to confiscate all precious metals except those used in wedding bands.[54] In his words, it was necessary "to restore to the Republic the wealth that had been obtained through malevolence and usurious monopolies."[55]

Indicative of his success, he had many confiscated metals melted down to make guns. As early as September 11, he sent off one hundred thousand gold marks to the Convention. On October 18, the Convention received twelve hundred pounds of Allier bar gold and 1,081 marks of ten-ounce silver. On October 29, he sent seventeen packing cases of chalices and chasubles to Paris.[56] Telling the Convention that the only things a true republican desired were "bread and iron," he exhorted: "Let us trample these idols of the Monarchy in the dust beneath our feet if we wish to secure adoration for the gods of the Republic and to establish the worship of liberty's stern virtues."[57]

In a festival on September 29 in honor of the elderly poor, Fouché urged people to make their own revolution: "If you lack flour; take it from the rich aristocrats, they have it; if you lack wheat, organize your own People's army and bring those *fermiers* and landowners to the scaffold who rebel against your requisitions; if you lack lodging, take the mansions belonging to your prisoners. . . ."[58] He thus told men and women to undertake actions they had been engaged in since 1790, but now he put the revolutionary government in Paris behind them.

His most dramatic projects in the Allier officially aimed to solve the grain crisis. Ideologically they functioned to define grain merchants and landowners as enemies of the People. On October 8, he urged popular societies to identify those who deliberately aimed to starve the *sans-culottes*. Those identified were to be publicly displayed on a scaffold under a sign proclaiming "*Affameur du peuple, traitre à la patrie* (Starver of the People, traitor to the country)."[59]

In one of his last actions in the Allier and the Nièvre before moving to Lyon, Fouché launched a civic festival to Courage and Morals on the first day of the first *décade* of the second month of Year II (October 22, 1793).[60] It was held in the plain of Plagny, in the Nièvre. One hundred and fifty tents surrounded an artificial mountain decorated with poplars, the usual liberty trees. Nearby, a sacred flame burned to Vesta, the Roman goddess of the public and private hearth. In groves on the plain, temples were constructed to Liberty, Love, and the Tables of the Law.

Cannons were fired at the Place Brutus at 5:00 A.M. to announce this new holiday in the secular calendar of the Revolution. The army drilled until eleven o'clock, when it moved to the "mountain." There, vinegrowers and barrelmakers drank wine with soldiers to demonstrate the equality of all. They marched past the temple of Love, kissing their weapons, and then past the constitutional arch toward the temple to the Tables of the Law, where Fouché read the Declaration of the Rights of Man and the Citizen. They continued their procession until they reached the Column of Liberty, where they sang more songs.

After seven rounds of cannonfire, newly married men arrived with their wives dressed in white. Children followed, dressed in white but wearing tricolored ribbons. Everyone then joined them for a procession of ordinary people. A cavalry brigade led the group followed by a chariot containing children dressed to represent the Graces, games, and laughter. Behind them marched the newlyweds, followed by adolescents and citizens who had adopted either children or old people. These citizens, in turn, were followed by women who breastfed their children, and other groups of older men and women. Another cavalry brigade took up the rear. Although a procession framed by cavalry suggests militaristic overtones, the official report of the festival indicates that in the march, images of games and pleasures of love overcame an image of war.

At this juncture, everyone left the chariots and joined a circle around the mountain. Fouché arrived and took his place at the top. After songs were sung to honor marriage, the newlyweds swore that their love was as eternal as that between Philémon and Baucis, the devoted couple of ancient mythology. They were then led to the temple of Love, where Fouché gave a speech followed by professions of "sacred love for the country." After the formal ceremony, officials served everyone "a frugal republican banquet." Crowds then adjourned to "the spectacle room" where they danced and sang for the rest of the evening.[61]

The festival stressed Fouché's desire to promote the republican family based on love and happiness, as well as love for the state. The oath to the relatively obscure Philémon and Baucis is particularly interesting. This mythological couple lived in the Phrygian hill country, where the gods Jupiter and Mercury, disguised as mortals, sought to determine the generosity of the region's inhabitants. Only the poorest — Philémon and Baucis — gave them food and shelter. To repay them for their generosity, Jupiter and Mercury advised them to *climb a mountain.* Near the summit, they watched as the gods flooded the Phrygian plain, destroying those who had refused to feed them. When told that they could have anything they wanted, this couple asked to die together. The gods allowed them to live as a happy family until very old, then turned them into trees, so they could stand together forever.

The festival demonstrates the extent to which revolutionary discourse blurred boundaries between public and private: the survival of the state depended on the generosity or virtue of the republican family based on love. The sacred flame burned in honor of Vesta, the goddess of the hearth, the symbol of the home. There seems no doubt that Fouché intended to emphasize the Rousseauian notion of the republican family as the source of "sacred love for the state."[62] Other messages also seem apparent. Philémon and Baucis were poor people — like sharecroppers and day laborers — who would feed and care for others in spite of their own poverty. They loved others out of both social consciousness and love for each other. One can also recognize the representation of hoarders and speculators in the selfish Phrygians, who refused to feed the gods and, hence, had to be destroyed. Phrygia was not just a land of hoarders, however, but also the name of the red hat associated with the freed slave, the hat that symbolized the radical Jacobins — the People — of the Revolution. Indeed, the shapeless red or Phrygian cap, along with Hercules, was arguably the most important symbol of the radical movement in the Revolution.[63]

This entire festival, unlike Fouché's earlier efforts, is pregnant with meaning. Ambiguous references cloud the allegory, however, making its message contradictory. Many classical references used must have been so obscure that very few understood them, yet there is very little verbal commentary added. Fouché deliberately left his symbols open to interpretation. More significant, he knew well enough that he could not be the Supreme Being; nonetheless, he placed himself ceremonially at the top of the mountain.

At this moment, Fouché recognized the ambiguity in his own project. He may have understood the necessity of destroying Phrygians/hoarders to enable his republican families to live harmoniously in his new society. Perhaps he realized that Reason alone was not enough, in spite of the care he exercised in making his festivals perfect. In any case, his festival promoted a General Will grounded in courage and morality — a will that could survive only by ending the lives of those who threatened it.

CENTRAL FRANCE IN THE WAKE OF THE TERROR

In assessing Fouché's influence, one must examine rural rebellion after his arrival. Rural men and women clearly followed Fouché in carrying out their own festive activity. Both Bourbon l'Archambault and Ygrande in the Allier held festivals in honor of the Supreme Being on 20 Prairial Year II (June 8, 1794). Their festivals copied Fouché's, but they added their own elements. Most interesting, the Popular Republican Society of Ygrande incorporated animals into their festival. This was completely outside of the official script, and the district government feared that the popular society was mocking official festivals. The society developed serious justifications for the animals, however: they honored the ox, without which cultivation would suffer; the goat, which reminded them of the milk that nourishes humans living in nature; the cow, which symbolizes the milk that nourishes people living in society; the sheep, which is used to clothe man.[64] At once, the Ygrandais employed the Rousseauian distinction between nature and society, but they emphasized how they worked, ate, and clothed themselves. They thus symbolized daily activities with animals, without references to classical figures. They intended to let everything speak for itself and only described what their symbols meant when challenged by the government. The juxtaposition of animals and concepts without words to control their meaning, then, was ambiguous enough to worry authorities.

Other rural actions also may have been stimulated by Fouché's exhortations. Popular societies followed Fouché in organizing banquets promoting egalitarianism. To illustrate the new order, they would have victims cook and serve them copious meals, and then remain standing while they ate.[65] Fouché also encouraged spying on everyone. Men and women went on expeditionary forces to ensure that everyone was supporting the Revolution.[66] Popular expeditions destroyed châteaux in Cérilly as signs of feudalism and despotism.[67] Denunciations became common.

We have no idea how many were arrested by Peoples' armies, although "cart loads" of prisoners were reportedly brought to Moulins.[68] In the Allier, one person was arrested for having told a revolutionary committee: "Ba, ba, your Convention has beautiful things to say, but the grain merchants are still our masters. . . ."[69] Another in Cusset was exposed because "he did not have an opinion on any of the major issues of the day."[70] In this dichotomous world of vice and virtue, to have no opinion implied vice, hence, treason.

Most suspects were involved with more serious "crimes" involving the grain trade. No matter how many festivals were organized, there was not enough grain to feed everyone. Restrictions on free trade prevented any from coming from other areas. Only armed force kept markets provisioned. Moreover, the creation of dispersed People's armies allowed many small communities to enter into neighboring territory to "requisition" food.[71] Such actions were legitimized as "official" business fostered by Fouché, but they were nearly identical to actions taken before Fouché arrived.

Encouraged by Fouché, riots also began to break out, as grain shortages underscored the contrast between urban and rural interests. Although rural workers — consumers themselves — frequently supported *sans-culottes* grain policies, sharecroppers were in an ambiguous situation. Whatever imaginary unity of will was achieved in festivals, it quickly fell apart once people acted in their own name. There was no real solution to the problem. To the extent that urban revolutionaries succeeded in enforcing the Maximum, the entire rural population, including sharecroppers and wage laborers, suffered. Without it, all workers, including many sharecroppers, could not eat.

On the other hand, rebellion in central France never ceased to resemble "class" warfare. Most of those arrested were *notables:* politicians, financiers, grain merchants, royal judges, nobles, and priests. An Allier revolutionary named Verd was accused of pursuing exclusively the bourgeoisie and village *messieurs.* The revolutionary Marat Chaix, of the Nièvre, hoped that "'his' *sans-culottes* could be used as a class weapon against *les gros* and *les bourgeois.*"[72]

In Year III, authorities in the Corbigny region bordering the Nièvre and the Allier explained that "insinuations by anarchists, spreading through all the districts, promising a carve-up of major properties, particularly the wooded land, and preaching insurrection against the rich or those said to be such" encouraged sharecroppers to violate agreements in their leases.[73] In a January, 1794, petition from the popular society of Brutus-le-Magnanime in (Saint-Pierre-le-Moûtier), villagers claimed that while the constitution guaranteed equality, the Revolution was allowing *fermiers* to develop large fortunes. Exercising rural logic, they argued that the only way the constitution could thus be upheld was "to prohibit large farms."[74]

In short, it is apparent that neither the festivals nor the Terror in this period were ever separated from the contradictions in the radical Montagnard program articulated in the Constitution of 1793. Both were designed to achieve equality, but the abstract principle of equality meant nothing when real material conditions based on access to private property divided revolutionaries on fundamental grounds. As a consequence, accusations increased, with all sides "speaking in the name of the People."[75]

While most of those denounced in a list of traitors from the small town of Cusset, in the Allier, were labeled "aristocrats," a careful examination of the accused demonstrates that most were either sharecroppers or bourgeoisie. Some of the bourgeoisie may have been acquiring national lands. All of the sharecroppers and workers (*manoeuvriers*) were accused of halting grain shipments or of other violations of the Maximum.[76]

It seems that after Fouché's arrival, in the popular language one had to be an aristocrat to be accused. In the process, all victims became "aristocrats" in the popular mentality, further reinforcing the belief in the existence of an aristocratic plot to starve the poor. Rhetorically, nonaristocrats could not be enemies of the People; hence, they had to be elevated in status. Language was thus used to minimize the differences revolutionaries refused to acknowledge.

This use of language may have permitted Fouché to contain popular rebellion by blurring the fairly distinct class lines drawn by sharecroppers and day laborers. Up until 1793, very little protest in the Allier and the Nièvre was directed against feudalism, seigneurialism, or aristocrats. On the contrary, most focused on *fermiers*, grain merchants, and the bourgeoisie. By subsuming these individuals into the common category of "aristocrat," Fouché was able to preserve the universality of Montagnard claims.

While many of those arrested for interfering with the grain trade were released, it increasingly became apparent that the market system was crumbling throughout France, multiplying the little revolts that broke out in places like the Allier and the Nièvre. Price controls eventually collapsed, but persons with grain continued to withhold it from market. Sharecroppers remained in the most ambiguous position of all, desperately in need of selling grain but materially in circumstances which barely differentiated themselves from rural wage labor. In this context, the *assignats* became completely worthless, despite Fouché's efforts to take precious metals out of private hands.

It was in this context, too, that Robespierre passed his infamous law of 22 Prairial (June 11, 1794) that allowed the accused to be executed without trial. Many revisionist historians have failed to recognize the social context of this action. They argue that the counterrevolutionary areas had been largely pacified and the foreign war was not going badly. They have not recognized the fiscal and moral collapse of a state that could market grain only at the point of a gun, once it admitted the desirability of a politics which promoted equality and guaranteed people the right to eat.

Thus, none of the festivals in central France was ever completely divorced from the class conflict inherent in everyday life. Unlike the gods Jupiter and Mercury, Joseph Fouché could not eliminate all those who refused to feed strangers or even their neighbors. He could not guarantee that wage earners would eat on any given day. Because he could not solve these problems without attacking the social structure in its entirety, violence intended to collectivize people instead polarized men and women in unintended ways.

These festivals and executions of Year II, then, hardly represent the kind of authoritarian rule pessimistically described by historians like Furet. The limited unity of central France was grounded in actions which genuinely depended upon a People's government ruling for the People, for Fouché's People's armies and committees constituted an extreme form of direct popular democracy that he could not control. In a sense, Fouché merely gave villagers a legitimacy and vocabulary for actions that would have been taken anyway. At the same time, the actions of men and women in central France moved Fouché in unintended directions, as he attempted to speak in their name. Assuming that similar processes transformed the deputies' intentions elsewhere, one can conclude that a great deal of political diversity existed within the fictive unanimity represented in the revolutionary politics of Year II.

Politics during the Terror appeared to be, as Furet argued, "a matter of establishing just *who* represented the People, or equality, or the nation: victory was in the hands of those who were capable of occupying and keeping that symbolic position."[77] Fouché better than most demonstrated that "revolutionary activity par excellence was the production of a maximalist language through the intermediary of unanimous assemblies mythically endowed with the General Will."[78] But Fouché, the political activist — unlike Furet, the historian — recognized the ambiguity inherent in this situation.

One can witness this ambiguity in Fouché's own apparently contradictory account of his role in the Terror. On the one hand, he differentiates his policy from the divisiveness of that of the Girondins, arguing that he was convinced "that there was no safety for the state but in the unity and indivisibility of the body politic."[79] He explains that violence was necessary and likened himself to Brutus, who had to sprinkle his children's blood to create the Roman republic. The King had to be killed "to inspire the representatives and the mass of the People with an energy sufficient to surmount the difficulties of the crisis [of 1792]." In other words, Hercules had to be made. Yet he also lamented his role in the king's execution and complained that he was "forced to employ the language of the times, and to yield to the fatality of circumstances. . . ."[80]

In his memoirs, Fouché argues that he was caught in quicksand from the moment revolutionaries attacked private property, when Hercules cried out, believing that the Revolution had betrayed him. Refusing to accept his own role in encouraging people to confiscate the property of émigrés, Fouché wrote after the Revolution that it was from the time that property was challenged that "the Revolution was nothing but a scene of ruin and destruction."[81] In his own mind, he could do little to stop the chaos, since his power was severely limited both by his superiors, who reduced him to a "man-machine" and by "*everyday phrases expressed in the language of the times.*" The problem with this language, he wrote, was that it was "official and peculiar."[82] He does not elaborate on what he means here, but one can guess. Forced to employ the official language of vice and virtue, aristocrats and People, one could never really confront difficult political problems as they were posed in the heat of revolution.

In the end, then, Fouché implicitly acknowledged that the myth of republican unity depended upon the idea of plots to emphasize the strength of the will of the People against well-defined enemies. That so many suspects were defined as aristocrats in spite of their social status underscores the significance of the ideology. Mythic unity, in other words, depended upon plots, which, in turn, necessitated that the Terror define the opposition as outside of, indeed, *before* the creation of the new republic.

To construct a revolution wherein the aristocracy, however vacuous its content as a category, lies outside of legitimate political identity is to construct a bourgeois revolution ideologically. Herein lay the difficulty for many revolutionaries, since the construction of the ideology left the bourgeoisie with no ground on which to define their own legitimacy except as "People," whereas many of the sharecroppers and day laborers emphatically denied that the bourgeoisie could be one with them. Speaking in the name of the People, hence, became increasingly problematic and increasingly dependent upon the Terror. The language of aristocratic plots and the exercise of the Terror, thus, were used to hold the Revolution together when real social cleavages threatened to fragment the General Will and tear the Revolution apart. The Terror was not then inherent in democratic politics per se, but only in their specific formulation during the radical phase of the Revolution, which aimed to deny both in discourse and in practice that social grievances could exist.

For a moment, the Revolution promised hope to some men and women who believed that greater equality was not only desirable but possible. They effected a total revolution on their own terms. This revolution articulated a politics of the People grounded in a social equality that revalued work and the fruits of labor while condemning the bourgeoisie, *fermiers*, and the national state as parasites. Fouché could not speak in the name of these people without reshaping his own politics to admit that social cleavages radically undermined any real General Will. In the process, the course of the Revolution was altered inexorably. Neither the abstract General Will nor the new political culture, in other words, was monolithic. Rather, they represented the product of many dialogues between Paris and the provinces and between the deputies of the National Convention and the awe-inspiring monster, the People acting in its own name.

NOTES

Funds for released time to prepare this article were provided by California State University. I wish to thank Jim Lehning, Leila Zenderland, and the Los Angeles Social History Group for their thoughtful comments on this manuscript. I am especially grateful to Sheldon Maram for his discussion of the argument and his extremely helpful critique of this text.

1. Archives départementales de l'Allier (hereafter cited as ADA), M.d.52, "Rapports sur les récoltes, 1814–1846."

2. Louis Biernawski, *Un département sous la Révolution française (L'Allier de 1789 à L'An II)* (Moulins, 1909), 291–94.

3. Georges Rougeron, "La période révolutionnaire et impériale," in *Nouvelle histoire du Bourbonnais des origines à nos jours*, ed. André Leguai (Le Coteau, 1985), 405–409; L. Audiat, *La terreur en Bourbonnais*, (Moulins, 1873–1893), I, 9–46; L.-J. Alary, "Fouché de Nantes à Moulins: Episode de la Terreur en Bourbonnais, 26 septembre 1793–14 février 1794)," *Bulletin de la Société d'émulation de l'Allier* (1861): 169–95. The same theme runs throughout Cornillon's volumes on the Revolution: Jean Cornillon, *Le Bourbonnais sous la Révolution française*, 5 vols. (Vichy and Riom, 1888–95), and *La vente des Biens nationaux*, 3 vols. (Moulins, 1911–13).

4. Nils Forssell, *Fouché: The Man Napoleon Feared*, trans. Anna Barwell, reprint (New York, 1970), 19–53; Louis Madelin, *Fouché, 1759–1820*, 2 vols. (Paris, 1900), I, 1–61; Nicole Bossut, "Aux origines de la déchristianisation dans la Nièvre: Fouché, Chaumette, ou les Jacobins Nivernais?" *Annales historiques de la Révolution française* 264, 2 (1986): 181–202; Norman Hampson, *A Social History of the French Revolution* (Toronto, 1963), 201–205; Gwyn A. Williams, *Artisans and Sans-Culottes: Popular Movements in France and Britain during the French Revolution* (New York, 1969), 56.

5. I deal with these themes in more depth in my forthcoming book on this topic. See also, Nancy Fitch, "Class Struggle in the Countryside: Social Change and Politics in Central France, 1200–1914" (Ph.D. diss., U.C.L.A., 1985), 409–507; Dr. De Brinon, *Vaumas* (Moulins, 1935), 122–23.

6. D. M. G. Sutherland, *France, 1789–1815: Revolution and Counterrevolution* (Oxford, 1985), 210–11.

7. "Proceedings of the Convention," July 2, 1793, in *Archives parlementaires*, LXVIII, 73. I was alerted to this reference after reading Lynn Hunt, *Politics, Culture, and Class in the French Revolution* (Berkeley; 1984), 101. See also Lynn Hunt, "Hercules and the Radical Image in the French Revolution," *Representations* 2 (1983): 95–117.

8. Hunt, *Politics*, 101.

9. Ibid., 106.

10. Mona Ozouf, *Festivals and the French Revolution*, trans. Alan Sheridan (Cambridge, Mass., 1988).

11. François Furet, *Interpreting the French Revolution*, trans. Elborg Forster (Cambridge, Eng., 1981).

12. Colin Lucas, *The Structure of the Terror: The Example of Javogues and the Loire* (Oxford, 1973).

13. Peter M. Jones, *The Peasantry in the French Revolution* (Cambridge, Eng., 1988), 232.

14. Georges Lefebvre, *Questions agraires au temps de la Terreur*, 2nd ed. (La Roche-sur-Yon, 1954), 91.

15. Ibid., 91–114; Serge Aberdam, "La révolution et les luttes des métayers," *Etudes rurales* 59 (1975): 73–91; T. J. A. LeGoff and D. M. G. Sutherland, "Religion and Rural Revolt in the French Revolution: An Overview," in J. M. Bak and G. Benecke, eds., *Religion and Rural Revolt: Papers Presented to the Fourth Interdisciplinary Workshop on Peasant Studies, University of British Columbia, 1982* (Manchester, 1984), 123–45.

16. Archives Nationales (hereafter cited as AN) H[1] 1453. "Emeutes"; AN F[1b] II Allier I, "Personnel du ministère"; AN F[1c] III Allier 9, "Esprit publique et les élections, Allier"; AN F[10] 284, "Comités d'agriculture des assemblées: pétitions, 1789–An III"; ADA L.54 and L.55, "Délibérations de l'Assemblée administrative du Département"; ADA L.60, "Délibérations du Directoire et de l'Administration centrale du Département."

17. Cornillon, *Biens nationaux*, II, 21–33.

18. Ibid., I, 42–54.

19. Fouché, "Citoyens mes collègues," Nevers, August 29, 1793, in Martel, [Le comte de], *Etude sur Fouché et sur Le communisme dans la pratique en 1793* (Paris, 1873), 118–19.

20. Bossut, "Aux origines de la déchristianisation," 188–89.

21. Ibid., 189–90.

22. AN F[10] 284; AN F[10] 320, "Comités d'agriculture des assemblées: pétitions, 1789–An II"; AN F[10] 212 B, "Doléances de plusieurs métayers et vignerons de Billy," June 13, 1790.

23. Antonin Besson, *Le destin d'une châtellenie: Billy-en-Bourbonnais* (Moulins, 1968), 470–71.

24. Lefebvre, *Questions agraires*, 110n.

25. I am grateful to Steven G. Reinhardt for helping me to clarify this argument.

26. Ovide Delaunay, "La vie économique: Les lois du maximum," in *Etudes sur la Révolution française dans l'Allier* (Moulins, 1945), 117–20.

27. Ibid.; "Grand, le représentant chargé de la levée en masse dans l'Indre et la Creuse au Comité de Salut Public," September 6, 1793, *Recueil des actes du Comité de Salut Public avec la correspondance officielle des représentants en mission et le regis-tre du Conseil Exécutif provisoire* (hereafter cited as RACSP), ed. F.-A. Aulard, VI, 315–16; R. R. Palmer, *Twelve Who Ruled: The Year of the Terror in the French Revolu-tion* (New York, 1969), 130–52.

28. Delaunay, "Maximum," 121–28, 174.

29. Marguerite Rebouillat, "La disette des grains dans le district de Cérilly (Allier) (1789–1795)," *Actes du 90ème Congrès Historique*, Nice, 1965, vol. II: *Section d'his-toire moderne et contemporaine* (Paris, 1966), 117–48.

30. Ovide Delaunay, "La Révolution française dans l'Allier (Août 1792–Septembre 1793," *Notre Bourbonnais* (10e Série, No. 219, 1er trimestre, 1982): 31.

31. J.-M. Lechevin, *Buxières-les-Mines: Petite cité laborieuse au coeur du bocage Bourbonnais*, vol. 1, *Histoire civile et religieuse* (Moulins, 1978), 200.

32. "Extrait du registre de la municipalité du Theil: séance du 12 mars 1793," reprinted in Le Lieutenant-Colonel Dulac, *Les levées départementales dans l'Allier sous la Révolution (1791–1796)*, (Paris, 1911), I, 311–15.

33. Lechevin, I, 200.

34. Delaunay, "Révolution française," 31.

35. Fouché to the Committee of Public Safety, Nevers, October 13, 1793, RACSP, VII, 402–403.

36. My emphasis. Joseph Fouché, "Aux habitants du département de la Nièvre," July 31, 1793, in Martel, *Etude sur Fouché*, 99–101.

37. Ibid., 101–103.

38. Furet, *Interpreting the French Revolution*, 71–72.

39. Fouché to the Committee of Public Safety, Nevers, August 3, 1793, RACSP, V, 466–67; Fouché to the Committee of Public Safety, Nevers, August 9, 1793, RACSP, V, 519–20.

40. Joseph Fouché, "Aux citoyens du département de la Nièvre," August 25, 1793, and Fouché to the Committee of Public Safety, August 29, 1793, in Martel, *Etude sur Fouché*, 113–19. Both documents are summarized but not reproduced in RACSP, VI, 108, 177.

41. Fouché to the Convention, Clamecy, August 17, 1793, RACSP, VI, 17; Fouché to the Committee of Public Safety, La Charité, September 13, 1793, in Martel, *Etude sur Fouché*, 129–31; Fouché to the Committee of Public Safety, La Charité, September 13, 1793, RACSP, VI, 475; Bibliothèque Nationale (hereafter cited as BN) Lb[41] 3256, "Pièces relatives à la mission du citoyen Fouché . . . pour ramener le calme et faire triompher le patriotisme dans le district de Clamecy et de Nevers, 1793"; BN Lb[40] 2728, "Procès-verbaux des séances des sociétés populaires du La Charité et de Nevers, tenues en présence de Fouché, Nevers, 1793."

42. "Séance publique des autorités constituées et de la Société populaire de Nevers," September 22, 1793, in Martel, *Etude sur Fouché*, 137–48.

43. Ibid., 149–52, Joseph Fouché, "Aux nom du Peuple français," September 22, 1793. The two men and the woman executed were accused of committing murder. They were not political prisoners. While evidence suggests that they were almost certainly guilty, Fouché seems to have rushed through their conviction so he could have three heads for his festival.

44. Ibid., 139, "Séance publique . . . de Nevers," September 22, 1793. Fouché's emphasis.

45. Ibid., 137–48.

46. Dorinda Outram, "*Le langage mâle de la vertu:* Women and the Discourse of the French Revolution," in Peter Burke and Roy Porter, eds., *The Social History of Language* (Cambridge, 1987), 120–35.

47. Bossut, "Aux origines de la déchristianisation," 200.

48. Cornillon, *Le Bourbonnais*, IV, 62–65.

49. ADA L.107, "Séance publique du 26 Septembre 1793, L'An II."

50. Ibid.

51. Ibid.; AN F[1c] III Allier 9.

52. ADA L.107.

53. Ibid.

54. Ibid.

55. AN F[1c] III Allier 9.

56. Forssell, *Fouché*, 66–67; Fouché to the National Convention, Nevers, October 18, 1793, RACSP, VII, 497; Fouché, October 18, 1793, *Réimpression de l'Ancien Moniteur* (Paris, 1863), XVIII, 172; Fouché to the Convention, October 29, 1793, RACSP, VIII, 113–14.

57. Forssell, *Fouché*, 66–67.

58. Delaunay, "La vie économique," 138; ADA L.107, "Séances des 29 et 30 septembre, 1793."

59. Fouché's emphasis. Joseph Fouché, "Aux citoyens du département de l'Allier," October 8, 1793, in Martel, *Etude sur Fouché*, 181–88.

60. BN Lb[41] 3427, "Fête civique pour honorer la valeur et les moeurs, arrêtée par le citoyen Fouché."

61. Ibid.

62. On this theme, see Joan B. Landes, *Women and the Public Sphere in the Age of the French Revolution* (Ithaca, 1988).

63. James Epstein, "Understanding the Cap of Liberty: Symbolic Practice and Social Conflict in Early Nineteenth-Century England," *Past and Present* 122 (February, 1989): 75–118; E. H. Gombrich, "The Dream of Reason: Symbolism of the French Revolution," *British Journal of Eighteenth Century Studies* 2 (1979): 195–96; Jennifer Harris, "The Red Cap of Liberty: A Study of Dress Worn by French Revolutionary Partisans, 1789–1794," *Eighteenth Century Studies* 14 (1981).

64. C. Grégoire, *Monographies révolutionnaires: département de l'Allier*, vol. 1: *L'ancien canton d'Ygrande (Ygrande, Bessais, St.-Aubin, St.-Plaisir, Vieure)* (Moulins, 1893), 42–45, and vol. 4: *L'ancien canton de Bourbon (Bourbon, Couzon, Franchesse, Le Breuil)* (Moulins, 1896), 119.

65. AN F[1b] II Allier I; Cornillon, *Biens nationaux*, II, 39–43.

66. *Réimpression de l'Ancien Moniteur*, October 27, 1793, XVIII, 195.

67. ADA L.109, "Les représentants du peuple en mission: Claude-Lazare Petit-Jean."

68. AN F[1c] III Allier 9.

69. ADA L.842, "Comité de Gannat, séance du 21 Messidor An II."

70. "Liste des individus arrêtés par ordre du Comité de Surveillance de Cusset," Cusset, An III, partially reprinted in Audiat, *La terreur*, I, 339–45.

71. ADA L.850, "Comité de surveillance du département de l'Allier, procès-verbaux des séances, 10 vendémaire an II–7 nivôse an II"; Cornillon, *Le Bourbonnais*, III, 171–73; IV, 24; Besson, 534; Rebouillat, 117–48; E. Delaigue, "A Saint-Menoux pendant la Révolution: les subsistances," *Bulletin de la Société d'émulation du Bourbonnais* 14 (1906): 227–39, 262–78.

72. Richard Cobb, *The People's Armies*, trans. Marianne Elliott (New Haven, 1987), 392–93.

73. Ibid., 432.

74. AN F[10] 285, "Lettre de la Société Populaire de Brutus-le-Magnanime," 25 Nivôse An II.

75. Delaigue, "A Saint-Menoux," 227–39, 262–75.

76. "Liste des individus arrêtés . . . Cusset," in Andiat, *La terreur*, I, 339–45.

77. Furet, *Interpreting the French Revolution*, 48–49.

78. Ibid., 50.

79. Joseph Fouché, *Memoirs of Fouché*, ed. Leon Vallée (Paris, 1903), 11.

80. Ibid., 11–15.

81. Ibid., 7, 13.

82. Ibid., 14. My emphasis.

DONALD SUTHERLAND

The Revolution in the Provinces: Class or Counterrevolution?

THE NARRATIVE STRATEGIES most historians adopt to recount the events of the French Revolution are quite simple. True, the actual content of that strategy is nowadays a matter of some debate. It is no longer quite so easy to identify political factions with social classes or subclasses. No longer is it possible, in other words, to confound the revolutionaries of 1789 with a rising bourgeoisie. Nor can one explain the factional fights of the revolutionary decade involving the Monarchiens, the Feuillants, the Girondins, the Montagnards, the Thermidoreans, the Clichiens, the Directorals, the Brumairians — that long and exhausting list of defeated factions cast up as so many layers of sediment to dry, solidify, and finally fossilize the historical landscape — by identifying these groups with reactionary, progressive, higher, or lower subgroups of the bourgeoisie. The reason political groups are no longer envisaged as outcroppings of a class bedrock is that the classical interpretation of the origins of the Revolution has shattered. Thus, if the origin of the Revolution cannot be read as a manifestation of a robust, self-confident, ambitious and enlightened, yet frustrated bourgeoisie, the course of the Revolution after 1789 can hardly be read as a struggle between the nobility and bourgeoisie.

This reasoning in turn poses a serious problem for a narrative strategy of the Revolution because the themes of bourgeoisie vs. nobility, modern world vs. reaction have been used to explain both why the 1790s were so violent and why the violence lasted so long. The triumph of anti-Marxist revisionism places the author of any history of the period before a narrative vacuum. None of the new books which has appeared during the bicentennial has quite dared embrace the logical consequence of this vacuum, namely that the violence was all rather senseless. And they have not done so, I suspect, because a ready-made alternative lies to hand in the rehabilitation of the Enlightenment as a cause of the Revolution. So, as the social interpretation is called into question, explanations based on ideology and culture — with liberal attention paid to post-structuralism, semiotics, and anthropology, and to Michel Foucault, Jacques Derrida, and Clifford Geertz — have come to the fore.[1]

Historians being an individualistic lot, scholarly consensus on the role of culture in the Revolution is so far rather loose. William Doyle and John Bosher, for instance, both agree that the governing and social elites shared a common liberal and enlightened culture in 1789.[2] The aims of the liberal reformers of the monarchy and the work of the Constituent Assembly had a common affiliation in this shared culture. Simon Schama sees the relation of reform and revolution only slightly differently.[3] According to Schama, an essentially liberal and benign Old Regime was assaulted by an outside elite passionately committed to a politics of equality and therefore illiberalism. The historian who has inspired all of these interpreters is, of course, François Furet.[4] In this as in so many other things, Furet follows Alexis de Tocqueville's point that the Revolution represented the triumph of egalitarian language. The monarchy aided the process by undermining the society of orders; the philosophical societies, which were the forerunners of the Jacobins, delivered the final blow.

The origin of the Terror is the most important issue anyone can address about the course of the Revolution itself, and current explanations favor a cultural approach here as well. Doyle's dense narrative seems to privilege the importance of political decisions and their disastrous consequences above all else, but most other historians would nowadays see day-to-day politics as deriving from a more broadly defined and embracing political culture. Thus, Lynn Hunt sees the Terror resulting in part from the revolutionaries' obsession with expunging the past and living in what she calls the "mythic present."[5] With such chiliastic expectations, their politics was incapable of compromise; moreover, opposition of any sort was intolerable. For Bosher, two cultures, as it were, came together in 1789. For the rest of the period, a self-serving coterie of ideological fanatics drunk on Rousseauism played on the baser instincts of hunger, ignorance and envy of ordinary people, concocting a fatal combination that eventually overthrew the gentle liberalism of the early Revolution. For Schama, a crazed and destructive bloodlust lay at the heart of the Revolution from the beginning. With typical hyperbole he writes, "The Terror was merely 1789 with a higher body count."[6] Once again, Furet has had a great influence on many recent writers. For him, the central theme of the Revolution was not class or counterrevolution, but factional competition over the power to appropriate revolutionary discourse — what he terms the politics of "democratic egalitarianism." Therefore, the driving force of the Revolution was the inherent need to radicalize it, to make it "consistent with its discourse" so that through struggle "the purest form of that discourse was eventually brought to power."[7]

If one examines the assumptions underlying these explanations, one finds an implicit model of how revolutionary politics works. Politics is sufficient unto itself, or rather, its underlying dynamic is to be understood in terms of the application of a set of ideological or cultural principles. This is a rather incomplete view of revolutionary politics, but the claims of its proponents go even further. In Furet's view and in the hands of some of his followers, the various revolutionary crises were generated out of the requirements of the exclusionary ideology itself. Thus, very early on, the revolutionaries created the nefarious image of the bloated, parasitic aristocracy as a demagogic device. One of Furet's followers, Jean-Clément Martin, has even claimed that the Jacobins' penchant for seeking out pervasive conspiracies and inflating the strength of their enemies provoked them to exaggerate extravagantly the resistance to conscription in the west of France in March, 1793.[8] A heavy-handed and hysterical repression of some minor disturbances stimulated locals to defend themselves, and the result was the massive Vendean rising of 1793, the largest single counterrevolutionary outbreak the Revolution faced.

Politics as ideology then, is one assumption. A second assumption is that what matters is high politics. It is remarkable how much Schama relies on the memoir literature of the nineteenth century, how much space parliamentary debate occupies in Doyle, how many of the entries in Furet and Mona Ozouf's dictionary are given over to historiography, ideas and prominent individuals.[9] In other words, it is remarkable how much the Revolution viewed as cultural phenomenon turns out to be the culture of the powerful. This is fair enough, as far as it goes, but it hardly does justice to the culture of ordinary people even in Paris, let alone the forgotten provinces, and it scarcely tries to cap-ture the experience of a decade of revolution for men and women throughout France.

This is the long road to the provincial history of the Revolution, but the route is justified. Provincial history should not be seen, as it so often is, as virgin territory for the apprenticeship represented by the Ph.D. thesis or the *doctorat*, or as kind of faraway summer lightning, whose flashes cast a distant illumination on the central events in Paris. Far from being backdrop, provincial history is central: all the major crises of the Revolution occurred in the provinces and the destiny of the Revolution was also determined there. Moreover, provincial reactions affected events in the national assemblies and even the Paris insurrections that so often form the narrative core of the period.

In a sense, the Revolution should have been over in 1789, to paraphrase the title of one of Furet's most famous essays. After all, by the end of the year, the Constituent Assembly had gone a long way toward meeting the national goal of the abolition of privilege. The list of reforms undertaken or promised was long and impressive: equality before the law, cheap justice, fiscal equality, religious toleration, strengthened property rights, equality of opportunity, citizen participation in government, abolition of the tithe and other ecclesiastical levies, and abolition of the most onerous or ubiquitous seigneurial dues without compensation. The list is perilously easy to enumerate by rote without realizing that in most circumstances many ordinary people's lives promised to be considerably easier and more humane as a result. This rosy picture has to be nuanced. It is equally easy to list the problems of transition: the difficulties of assuring fiscal equality in an agrarian society without a thorough land survey, a process which was not completed until well into the nineteenth century; the reneging, at least as some saw it, on the promise of thorough equality by imposing a property qualification on the vote; and the casuistical attempt to surround remaining seigneurial dues with the mantle of property rights. Yet historians perhaps dwell on these difficulties too much. Fiscal equality probably did not matter a lot when the combination of high inflation and poor administration gave ordinary people a tax holiday for much of the period. The demand for political equality was fairly limited, and one wonders how much it really mattered to the electorate when at best the turnout for elections, with or without a property qualification, was so spotty or so low—rarely more than forty percent in the elections of 1791 and declining to an abysmal ten percent or less in 1799. As for resistance to the remaining seigneurial dues, circumstances proved that politicians were unwilling to enforce the laws protecting the erstwhile lords' rights to collect. In any case, none of the anti-seigneurial riots of the early 1790s called the principles of 1789 into question. On some of the major issues of transition, therefore, circumstances proved that adjustments or compromises could be made with popular demands.

On other issues, however, the politicians were practically unanimous in refusing compromise, and one does not have to postulate an inner need of revolutionary ideology and culture to see why. Resistance to the religious reforms of the Revolution was real and it was dangerous. At first, this resistance caught politicians off guard. After all, the Civil Constitution of the Clergy, as the main package of religious reforms was called, in no way compromised central Catholic doctrines let alone liturgy, which historians of early modern Europe tell us is what ordinary people really cared about. Confiscating church property, abolishing the tithe, dissolving the contemplative orders, redrawing ecclesiastical boundaries, paying the clergy salaries, even the lay election of parish priests and bishops—none of these things challenged the intercessionary powers of the clergy or its ability to mediate with the supernatural or its timeless role as the focal point for community self-definition and worship. Many clerics themselves endorsed the Civil Constitution. Sixty percent of them took an oath of loyalty to it because as "citizen priests" they too were swept along in the general enthusiasm for the Revolution.[10]

Yet the schism between constitutional and refractory priests acquired the importance it did because each side was able to command lay support. Explaining this support is hardly as self-evident as nineteenth- and early twentieth-century historians thought it was. The older interpretation of self-interested counterrevolutionary priests manipulating the credulity of an ignorant laity simply appropriates the uncritical and simple analysis the revolutionaries themselves made of the problem: a discourse which permitted them simultaneously to dismiss popular oppositon and to isolate and repress the clergy. Yet, reading below this layer of revolutionary rhetoric in contemporary police documents allows the reconstruction of a popular mentality which was neither gullible nor ignorant. Instead we can see a frame of reference clustered around ideas of liturgy, community, purity and humanity. Ideas of this sort are difficult to articulate, but is is possible to move through several screens of complexity, all the while realizing that the logic we have to impose on the material for our own understanding probably gives an illusion of order to a more disconnected reality. Nonetheless, at the level of demands for liturgy, communication with people in the past is fairly clear.

Contemporary observers in the west of France tended to link the dispersed habitat of the region to the area's well-known religiosity. Church-going overcame the inherent loneliness of living in such isolation, and so religiosity and the church acquired an importance here that was hardly possible in the regions of grouped habitat along the northern plains. Napoleonic officials emphasized this element to justify reopening the churches because they fully intended to control lay public opinion via the clergy, a project which was impossible as long as formal church services were nonexistent.[11] Although country folk themselves deployed this argument, their petitions more commonly emphasized the importance of the administration of sacraments and *secours spirituels* generally.

Yet clearly there was more to this demand for liturgy, because the constitutional priests were as capable and as qualified to fulfill these functions as the refractory priests. Indeed, when communities had no priests at all after the forced deportations of the Terror, lay people conducted their own religious ceremonies. It was the constitutionals themselves who were the problem. The idea that one was arriving to replace the beloved refractory could set off waves of panic through entire communities.[12] Constitutionals were Protestants who hated the Virgin, it was said, their masses were sullied, their marriage ceremonies would result only in concubinage. There was a clear association throughout all this wild talk with concepts of purity and pollution. Thus moral purity in the sense of leading an exemplary life was ascribed to the refractories. Petitions emphasize how these priests lived up to the Counter-Reformation ideals of dedication, holiness, love of the poor, and a sense of duty. Constitutionals and their Jacobin allies did not inhabit the exact opposite place along this moral continuum so much as another space, which was dark and repulsive. Constitutional curés, it was said, made some people retch, Jacobins had a rotten smell, the devil was painted on their faces, their hearts were black like chimney soot, and when they died their bodies immediately blackened while those of "aristocrats" became "white like snow." People associated living under the ministry of a constitutional or living under no priest at all with living at the moral level of animals, beasts without souls.

The language of liturgy and purity existed alongside that of community, and this, in turn, permits us to link discourse to social structure and political events. The idea of community was a cultural construct like any other, but it permitted the expulsion of transgressors of community norms, no matter how long they had been actual physical residents.[13] It also provided a mechanism for readmission which closely resembled Catholic practices of contrition and penance. People who had gone too far had always been excluded, but in the Revolution this notion became politicized when it was applied to constitutional curés and their supporters. They all became *intrus* or intruders. A whole revolutionary vocabulary was similarly purged. Words like *citoyen, loi, nation, patrie*, which have a rather neutral charge nowadays, became associated with these factious outsiders. In other words, the reason the constitutional curés and their friends had the language of purity, revulsion, and unworthiness applied to them was that their independence was compromised. Whatever their original intention, the constitutional clergy embraced the role of citizen priest often with enthusiasm and courage. Public authorities, clubs, and National Guards not only applauded this activity, which they saw in missionary terms as efforts to shine the revolutionary light on ignorant rural masses, but *in extremis* were prepared to back it up with force.

Language thus articulated a social struggle between countryfolk and a largely urban bourgeoisie and their local artisan allies. This in turn was a function of the landholding structure and the effects of the Revolution on it. The general rule of thumb is that opposition broke out in regions where numerous and medium-sized leaseholders — whether sharecroppers, cash-paying farmers, or holders under exotic forms of tenure like *domaine congéable* or *complant* — dominated the local community. Men like these, whose security varied immensely from place to place, gained little or nothing from the economic reforms of the Constituent Assembly. Taxes were partially avoidable, but an immediate rise in rent which the assembly authorized to compensate for the defunct tithe brought little or no benefit to renters. Research in

estate papers in Upper Normandy and elsewhere suggests that landlords immediately exercised their rights to reopen leases and the tithe
was fully folded into the rent.[14] Population pressure on the land soon
snuffed out the effects of the abolition of seigneurial dues. By the late
1790s, taxes, which were far higher than those of the old monarchy,
had begun to bite so that rising rent curves leveled off but rarely fell.
In short, renters paid more than they ever had before.[15] Why should
they accept *la nation* and its failed promises? Why should they have
any confidence in its arrogant clergy who expected countryfolk to sub-
mit meekly to a regime that had distributed its benefits to such a narrowly defined and unrepresentative class of bourgeois landlords?

As it stands, this model works very well for the west of France,
that is, the old provinces of Normandy, Brittany, Maine, Anjou and
Poitou. It is also useful for understanding the genesis of opposition in
Flanders and Artois, where the landholding structure was different.
In these areas it took not only narrowly distributed economic reforms
but two years of undiscriminating terrorism, hysterical dechristianization, and ruthless requisitions to realign social forces within the villages to produce a quasi-counterrevolutionary opposition. Similarly,
opposition was slow to emerge in the southwest because alongside disillusioned sharecroppers who got nothing, there were as many small
owners who had reason to hope. Again, it took a combination of economic collapse and requisitioning to force communities to make
choices. The model does not appear to work at all, however, in the
lower Rhone Valley around Nîmes, where bloody sectarian violence
overrode the rational calculation of self-interest that contemporary
Physiocrats might have preferred.

The *bagarre de Nîmes* of May, 1790, and the consequent *camps
de Jalès* were appalling slaughters in which Catholics and Protestants
killed each other by the score in order to seize control of regional and
municipal governments. These incidents were hardly isolated. Throughout Upper Languedoc, Provence, Alsace, Flanders, and the west, local
politics revolved around the position of the constitutional priest. The
countless boycotts, stonings, disturbances, and riots were the first sign
that authority was noisily slipping from revolutionary authories. The
reaction of the broad revolutionary coalition showed that the first breakdown of the rule of law occurred not because of an abstract thirst for
equality but because the Revolution was faced with real enemies. In

the first place, local National Guards tried to intimidate the refractory priests and their supporters. Although these movements have never been properly charted, it is clear that throughout the west and the Midi the guards operated in several waves by closing down refractory churches, threatening their followers, or intimidating the refractories into taking the oath. The guard of Marseilles was on the move constantly, undertaking expeditions to confound real or imagined conspiracies in places as far away as Avignon, Orange, and Arles. By the late winter of 1793, they were no longer simply disarming their enemies but hanging them on village squares and extorting "revolutionary taxes" from villages unfortunate enough to have shown too much sympathy for a refractory priest.

Beyond some self-serving hand-wringing, public authorities did nothing to stop these marauders because, one has to suspect, they sympathized with the guards' aims. Certainly they had no more respect for the law or due process. From the spring of 1791, clubs, departments, and districts petitioned the National Assembly for a law exiling the refractories or interning them. Even without a law, departments interned priests in the aftermath of the king's abortive flight to Varennes. In November, 1791, and again in April, 1792, the Legislative Assembly finally did pass laws permitting exile or internment, only to have them vetoed by Louis XVI. The departments ignored the vetoes anyway. By June, 1792, at least forty-six departments were decreeing internal exile or limited arrest without trial of refractories. There was a chorus of justifications for these measures, but the administrators of the department of Maine-et-Loire spoke for all their peers when they claimed, "The measure is not in the law but the safety of the people is the supreme law."[16] Such arguments are also the essence of the terrorist mentality, a position derived not from abstract Rousseauian ideology, but from the fear of a dangerous and elusive enemy.

The bypassing of the king's veto shows how far royal authority had crumbled, but the veto itself convinced provincials that Louis XVI himself protected the internal enemy. The demand for Louis's deposition originated in the provinces. Not surprisingly, Marseilles stated it most boldly by claiming hereditary monarchy was incompatible with the Declaration of the Rights of Man and Citizen. Moreover, it was the provincial national guards or *fédérés* who proved decisive in the *journée* of August 10, 1792, which overthrew the monarchy. Nor should it be surprising that the most prominent contingents — those of Finistère and, of course, Marseilles — came from areas where the struggle against popular counterrevolution had been most acute. For them, the expedition to Paris was only the climax of the many expeditions they had undertaken for the previous two years.

It is easy to imagine that in the process described, there might be a paradigm for the provincial revolutions as a whole. The transitions in the narrative from local cultural traits and social structures to disturbances, to repression, to defiance of the national government, to the mobilization for its overthrow — these transitions seem rather simple to recount. Yet although there are numerous cases of how provincial problems eventually worked themselves into national politics, there are other elements which render the whole process exotic and often baffling. Perhaps the best way to illustrate this problem would be to examine that wonderful image we have inherited from the Revolution, the people in arms.

Everyone is familiar with it: French men and women, confronted with the danger of foreign invasion and internal subversion, sacrificed themselves for *la patrie*, unselfishly giving of their treasure, their bodies, and their labor to the ideal of nation and liberty. There is a great deal of truth in this, and no one would wish to trivialize such heroic sacrifices. But there is a more sophisticated way of conceiving of the mechanics of a revolutionary crisis, one that relies on another rule of thumb. As perils to the Revolution increased, it had to demand more and more of people, yet many of these people could see no very good reason why they should commit themselves. A crisis, far from rallying the nation, tended to enlarge the circle of the revolutionary government's enemies. It is possible to illustrate this most clearly by analyzing the crisis of 1793.

In February, 1793, the National Convention declared war on Great Britain and would soon declare war on Spain. The previous spring, war had broken out with Austria and Prussia, so that for the campaign of 1793, France could expect to be attacked on all its land and sea frontiers. The army was also in disarray. The problems of desertion from a largely aristocratic officer corps and the potential disloyalty of the remainder — combined with the low level of commitment of the volunteers, many of whom had simply returned home after the successful campaign of 1792 — made it clear that major reforms would have to be undertaken. One of the most important was the February 24 *levée* of three hundred thousand men. This made every young man between the ages of eighteen and twenty-five eligible for army service, a measure of conscription that even Louis XIV at the height of his power had not dared to impose on his kingdom.

The *levée* was the first time the fledgling Republic had asked for mass support, and, throughout the nation, the result was deeply disturbing. Young men subject to the draft stormed meeting halls, burned official papers, molested mayors, and ripped out liberty trees. In the west, resistance sparked off the Vendée rebellion, the most massive and dangerous of all the peasant risings of the Revolution. Here the young men's resentments were joined to generalized grievances about higher taxes, higher rents, and the Civil Constitution of the Clergy. Within a matter of a weeks, several regional centers like Cholet, Machecoul, La Rochebernard, and Guérande (among others) had fallen. By the end of March, republicans had repressed the troubles north of the Loire, but to the south of it, the various peasant bands, often under somewhat reluctant noble leaders, coalesced into a self-styled "Catholic and Royal Army of the West." From its increasingly secure base, the army launched successful attacks on Saumur and Angers and had come very close to taking Luçon and Nantes. At the same time, it sent off emissaries to England to demand military aid. To borrow the Jacobin phraseology, the internal and the external enemies were coming together.

Equally grave was the military situation along the northern frontiers. The renewal of the campaigning season brought defeats climaxing at Neerwinden on March 18. General Dumouriez then tried to blame the Jacobins for the defeats, arranged a truce with the Austrians, and intended to march his soldiers to Paris "to restore the sane part of the Convention." Unfortunately for him, the soldiers refused and he had to take refuge by fleeing to the Austrian lines with his men shooting at his galloping horse.

The Vendean rebellion and Dumouriez's treason are responsible for the passage of two of the most notorious laws of the period, whereas the interpretation that contemporaries put on the crisis is responsible for a third. In direct response to the risings in the West, the Convention passed the law of March 19, which required execution within twenty-four hours if a military commission found an accused guilty of having participated in an armed counterrevolutionary assembly. The

March 10 law establishing the Revolutionary Tribunal in Paris was a direct response to Dumouriez's treason. The tribunal was at first empowered to seek out and punish conspiracy in high places, but its purview soon widened to include political crimes of all sorts. The Revolutionary Tribunal reflected the widespread belief that internal treason was primarily responsible for the nation's woes. This same assumption underlay the establishment of the revolutionary committees by the law of March 21, 1793. At first, they had the power to arrest only foreigners or those without internal passports, but when the committees were assigned the Law of Suspects on September 17, 1793, they were authorized to intern anyone suspected of being an enemy of liberty — virtually anyone they wanted, in other words — or to denounce a suspect to the revolutionary tribunals or military commissions.

The crisis of March, 1793, forced the Convention to adopt many of the measures associated with the Terror. There were many others: imposing revolutionary taxes, mandating greater central intervention in the life of the departments, and directing a massive commitment to regulating the economy through price controls on the grain trade. These policies demanded a degree of compliance and enthusiasm from the citizenry that was not always forthcoming. Where these measures were actively resisted, the result was federalism.

Federalism is one of the most elusive movements of the period because so many of its aims were negative, and the federalists never established national or regional organizations. "Federalist" is a Jacobin epithet, and it has confused historians ever since into believing the federalists were decentralizing provincials and reactionaries. In fact, the federalists thought of themselves as the better-off sort defending themselves against a bloodthirsty cabal of teeth-gnashing Jacobins who would stop at nothing to institute their program of slaughter and envy. So, if federalism had a strong class-conscious element to it, it was also urban and, for the most part, confined to the cities of the southeast.

Without examining federalism city by city, one can enumerate many common factors. Most of the major cities had had an exceptionally violent history earlier, and Lyon, Bordeaux, Toulon, and the Marseilles region all had their equivalents of the Paris September massacres in which suspected enemies of the Revolution had been hauled from prison and murdered. The local Jacobin clubs, far from disavowing these atrocities, apologized for them and sometimes threatened a new round of killings of hidden enemies. The clubs also affected to represent the humble and the poor by unleashing a demagogic attack on any manifestation of wealth. The news from the frontiers and from the Vendée provoked the crisis within the cities. Quite often illegally, the Jacobins set about organizing conscription, raising revolutionary taxes and forced loans on the rich, rigging elections, disarming suspects, and establishing their own revolutionary committees, and did all this amid bloodcurdling threats against the moderates and the rich. For their part, the rich — always a rather loose category — believed the Jacobins were merely using the military crisis as a pretext to seize their property. Far from rallying to the nation at its moment of peril, the anti-Jacobins believed that a violent faction had seized the rudder of state — an interpretation applied to the national scene when the Jacobins and the Paris National Guard intimidated the Convention into expelling the Girondins on May 31–June 2, 1793.

Although the federalists were able to dislodge the Jacobins from the city halls of the southeast and institute a counterterror of their own, the federalist armies marching to Paris never amounted to much. But the whole federalist episode illustrates another essential axiom of revolutionary politics: that the revolutionary leadership had a fairly narrow social and political base, too narrow at any rate to command broad and unquestioning legitimacy in a crisis. Thus in the summer of 1793 the Revolution entered its gravest crisis. The elimination of the Girondins from the Convention had solved nothing. The military was falling back, the city of Mainz having to accept a humiliating surrender in July, Toulon surrendering itself to an Anglo-Spanish fleet in August, the federalist cities still in revolt, the Vendeans inflicting one victory after another upon a quarreling and dispirited republican army. Everyone knows how the Jacobins and the Committee of Public Safety turned this around. It is the stuff of any textbook, but I would like to examine a little-appreciated aspect of that struggle, dechristianization.

Dechristianization was part of a broad attempt to create a new civic moral order and, as such, was the climax of the chiliastic tendencies that had been present in the Revolution from the beginning. But dechristianizers also sensed the necessity of pushing these tendencies to their extreme; after four years of experience, they finally understood that the clergy had acquired and maintained its influence because popular culture was ubiquitously and profoundly Catholic and religious. Joseph Fouché, the most famous dechristianizing deputy of all and long before his descent into the worldly cynicism of being Bonaparte's minister of police, attributed the Vendean risings to "ignorance and fanaticism." The antidote was "public instruction . . . inspired by the revolutionary and clearly philosophical spirit [which alone] can offset the odious influence of religion."[17] The *agent national* of the district of Mâcon concurred. "Since the beginning of the Revolution," he wrote, "the Catholic cult has been the cause of many troubles. Under the cloak of religion, the progress of civic-mindedness has been much hampered. Disastrous wars have taken place. Would it not be appropriate to authorize only the cult of the Revolution?"[18]

The dechristianizers did not have time for systematic public instruction; their cults were little more than exotic improvisations. Indeed, theirs was a remarkably Catholic dechristianization with its martyrs of liberty, trinities of saints, republican relics (Marat's heart was suspended from the ceiling of the Cordelier Club), and apparitions of dead republican heroes. They were most effective at iconoclastic blasphemy: destroying relics before stupefied peasants and inviting a wrath which never came, ripping out roadside crosses, desacralizing cemeteries, and closing or even burning churches. Nor were these efforts as mindlessly vengeful as they might seem, for consciously or not, if the revolutionaries could show how ineffective the control of the supernatural over the natural was, then they would break one of the basic pillars sustaining peasant religion. Similarly, forcing the clergy to marry was akin to forcing the aristocracy to surrender its privileges in 1789: obliterate separate estates and there was no longer any reason to oppose the national will.

Dechristianization did not work, of course, but its failure illustrates a final point about the Revolution and the provinces. It is not simply that at the height of the dechristianization campaign, peasants in northern Burgundy attributed a hailstorm which destroyed their vines to the "disappearance of their priests and their stone saints," as one official disdainfully put it.[19] Nor is it that dechristianization provoked another round of processions, incantations, and nocturnal masses, which would continue through the post-Terror regimes until Bonaparte was forced to deal with popular religion by conceding the Concordat in 1802. The point is that however modern the principles of 1789 are, however much the Declaration of the Rights of Man and Citizen speaks to the world of 1989, for many French men and women of the eighteenth century, the Revolution was tragically and profoundly alien.

NOTES

1. There are two handy guides: J. G. Merquior, *Foucault* (London, 1985), and C. Norris, *Derrida* (London, 1987). Also see Clifford Geertz, "Religion as a Cultural System," in his *The Interpretation of Cultures* (New York, 1973), 87–125.

2. John F. Bosher, *The French Revolution* (New York, 1988); William Doyle, *The Oxford History of the French Revolution* (Oxford, 1989).

3. Simon Schama, *Citizens: A Chronicle of the French Revolution* (New York, 1989).

4. François Furet, *Interpreting the French Revolution*, trans. Elborg Forster (Cambridge, Eng., 1981).

5. Lynn Hunt, *Politics, Culture and Class in the French Revolution* (Berkeley, 1984), 26–28.

6. Schama, *Citizens*, 447.

7. Furet, *Interpreting the French Revolution*, 70.

8. Jean-Clément Martin, *La Vendée et La France* (Paris, 1987).

9. François Furet and Mona Ozouf, *Dictionnaire Critique de la Révolution française* (Paris, 1988), *passim*.

10. Timothy Tackett, *Religion, Revolution, and Regional Culture in Eighteenth-Century France: The Ecclesiastical Oath of 1791* (Princeton, 1986), 70–74.

11. See Paul Bois, *Paysans de l'Ouest* (Le Mans, 1960), 612–15.

12. This is a reinterpretation of the material in my *The Chouans. The Social Interpretation of Popular Counter-Revolution in Upper Brittany, 1770–1796* (Oxford, 1982), 214–18, 241–57, supplemented with Tackett, *Religion, Revolution and Regional Culture*, 166–68, 172–77.

13. Timothy J. A. Le Goff and D. M. G. Sutherland, "The Revolution and the Rural Community in Eighteenth-Century Brittany," *Past and Present* 62 (1974): 96–119.

14. Archives départementales, Seine-Maritime, 7J 37, 77, chartier de Clèves. More generally, Daniel Zolla, "Recherches sur les variations du revenu et du prix des terres en France. Deuxième partie (1789–1815)," *Annales agronomiques* 14 (1888): 49–78.

15. Timothy Le Goff and Donald Sutherland, "The Revolution and the Rural Economy," *Revue d'histoire moderne et contemporaine* (forthcoming).

16. Cited in D. M. G. Sutherland, *France, 1789–1815: Revolution and Counter-revolution* (Oxford, 1985), 137.

17. Cited in Louis Madelin, *Fouché, 1759–1820*, 2 vols. (Paris, 1900) I, 49.

18. Archives départementales de Saône-et-Loire, 2L 616.

19. Cited in Henri Forestier, "Les Campagnes de l'Auxerrois et la déchristianisation," *Annales de Bourgogne*, (1947): 191–92.